DOING& SAYING THE RIGHT THING

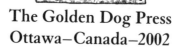

The Golden Dog Press
Ottawa–Canada–2002

© 2002 by Allan Bonner

ISBN 0-919614-98-1

Canadian Cataloguing in Publication Data

Bonner, Allan
    Doing and saying the right thing: professional risk and crisis
    management

Includes bibliographical references.
ISBN 0-919614-98-1

1.Risk management.   2.Crisis management.   3.Public relations.
I. Title.

HD61.B66 2001   658.15'5   C2001-904013-X

Layout and Cover Design: The Gordon Creative Group of Ottawa.

Manufactured in Canada.

Table of Contents

Acknowledgements

A book such as this is a result of many experiences, readings and discussions. As I begin writing the traditional few sentences to pay my debts, I am sure I will leave many delinquent accounts. Two professors stand out: P.J. Fitzpatrick at the University of New Brunswick who put a premium on clear argumentation and Simon Bennett at Leicester who coached me through my MSc. The early risk theorists, including Vince Covello and Peter Sandman, helped get me into a very specialized field early in the game. Then, Roger E. Kasperson's "social amplification of risk," and Ulrich Beck's "risk society" helped me take my theories farther.

Several clients helped as well. My travelling up to 150 days per year between 1987 and 1997 allowed me to try out my concepts on five continents in both hemispheres, during some challenging times. I am privileged to have travelled and worked with about 2,000 senior Canadian military officers at most Canadian bases, in Cyprus and at National Defence Headquarters in Ottawa. My work with our Department of Foreign Affairs and International Trade helped me hone my skills with ambassadors all over the world as well as with UN and G7 delegations. Several oil, gas and chemical companies got me into the simulation business after Valdez and Bhopal, for which I am grateful.

In short, I've been blessed with great academic and practical experiences.

This book began as a series of lectures I wrote and delivered to senior military officers near the end of the Cold War. I then recorded the lectures and turned them into an audio based distance learning programme. That script formed the nucleus of this book. I want to thank Hal Jones, my senior trainer and crisis counsellor, for reading several early drafts and suggesting many changes which added clarity and structure.

So, this has been in the works since 1987, and it's hard to remember all those who may have spurred me on or suggested a better way to express a concept. I am sure, though, that my wife, the nationally known broadcaster, Lorna Jackson, heard every concept several times at breakfast, over dinner and just before nodding off at night. She is a great issues manager who can get to the core of a problem instantly, or think of a concrete way to teach an ephemeral concept clearly. More importantly, she has shown great patience over the past 20 years.

Thanks to all, and, as they say, errors and omissions are mine.

Allan Bonner, BA, BEd, MA, MSc, PhD (Cand.)
Toronto, Canada

For media appearances, many spokespeople find the makeup chair intimidating.

"Communication" is one of the most commonly used — perhaps overused — words of the modern age.

Indeed, it is often said that this is the *communication* age. Few people in the world can remain isolated from what is going on in other parts of the world, even if they want to.

Words and pictures about events and ideas are conveyed around the globe in the blink of an eye. Information, in its broadest sense, has never been easier to come by. The Internet makes no distinction between fact and fiction.

Knowledge is today's most valued currency, and the ability to communicate that knowledge to good effect is a skill that is much sought after. Unfortunately, fewer people have that skill than *think* they have it.

The problem is one of familiarity. It is precisely because "communication" is such an everyday term that we don't pay it the attention it deserves and its impact is often diluted. Governments and institutions, businesses and private organizations all have departments and people dedicated to communicating their policies, values, beliefs and actions to others.

Those whose purpose is simply to transfer information or data from one place to another have an easily defined task and easily achieved objective. This book is not for them. The post office is more geared to that job.

Transferring information and data is not the same as communicating. The information, or message, you transmit has no value if it doesn't have an impact on the recipient, as minimal or transitory as that impact may be.

Many people are convinced that all they have to do to "communicate" is to speak or write in the language of the intended listener or audience. You don't have to try very hard to imagine all the things that can go wrong with that simplistic approach.

The main thing that goes wrong is the confusion of communication with transportation. The two are often in the same sections of geography texts. We study cities as centres of "transportation and communication," but that doesn't mean that the two items are the same thing. Transportation of messages can involve putting a message in an envelope, clicking "send" after writing an e-mail or reading a speech. But the recipient might not get the message, despite the reliability of the post office, computers and human ears. Just because the communicator spoke or wrote or clicked doesn't mean the recipient understood.

Most of us have had the misfortune to sit through a speech, or a business presentation, that made little or no sense to us, even though we understood most of the words and sometimes even whole sentences. Then there's the letter, memo or e-mail that seems as confusing on third reading as it did at first sight.

That's because the speaker or writer didn't try hard enough to communicate with us.

As a communicator, it is your responsibility to ensure your message is received and understood. If your audience doesn't get the point, or is confused, then you have failed to communicate.

There's no point in blaming your audience — even if you're the boss. You can't order people to understand you; you can only make it easier for them to understand you.

That's what this book is about.

The SOCKO™ system has already helped people in many parts of the world to be better communicators. It has proved its value in high-profile situations with politicians, diplomats, military leaders, trade negotiators and other public officials. It's also worked with business executives, police officers, lawyers and social institutions.

The SOCKO™ system is user-friendly both for communicators as well as their audiences.

The SOCKO™ system is the most powerful communications tool you will ever own.

Please take a look at the iceberg diagram which follows and please read the definition of a SOCKO™. If you list three short words or phrases you might have to speak about, the SOCKO™ system is beginning to work for you. You can also imagine that the iceberg is everything you know about a topic and start brainstorming about what that information is. Then you can try to imagine what the most important ten percent might be — or the tip of the iceberg.

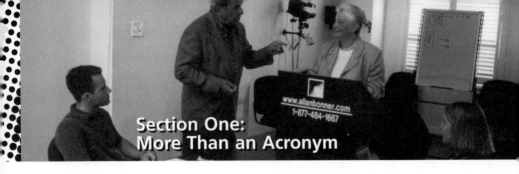
Many speakers are fearful behind a podium. SOCKOs™ and practice lessen the tension.

SŎCKÓ™

(sŏ ko´) n. acronym for Strategic Overriding Communications and Knowledge Objective. 1. A short, positive, sharp, memorable, honed, polished, true, unassailable statement. 2. A media-genic clip or quotation on radio, TV or in newspaper stories. 3. A 20-second or less, quotable quote, with impact, often showing caring, knowledge and/or action. 4. A rough equivalent to a headline, cutline or lead, best delivered after full rehearsal at least three times, e.g., I have nothing to offer but blood, toil, tears and sweat, ... ask not what your country can do for you; ask what you can do for your country... , just watch me ... .

1.

2.

3.

Figure 1: SOCKO™ Definition with Iceberg

The SOCKO™ Management System Will Change Your Life

I've seen it work for government leaders, diplomats, people who head multinational corporations, generals and people who work with homeless kids, so I know it will work for you.

This is a huge claim to make and I'm making it after putting 15,000 of the world's toughest clients through a variety of training courses based on the SOCKO™ system. We use SOCKOs™ in witness preparation, negotiation, presentation skills, managing meetings, media training, risk communication, crisis management and other cases where our clients have to communicate under pressure.

When you emerge from a courtroom, boardroom or war-room and start explaining "what went wrong" or describing a new policy, the next 10 seconds can have a profound effect on budgets, the regulatory environment and careers. SOCKOs™ just might be all that stands between you and a red face. SOCKOs™ can protect against lower share prices, investigations and damage claims.

SOCKO™ is a Way of Thinking

Once upon a time, our actions were governed by nothing more complicated than self-preservation and survival. There wasn't much thinking involved. Later, tribal and religious leaders provided us with strict rules about how to act. We pillaged the neighbouring village because it had pillaged ours or because their people had insulted our gods. Our actions still didn't need much thought.

One message of the renaissance, especially the message of Shakespeare's Hamlet, is the danger of reflection in lieu of action. Too much thinking and not enough acting can stifle a person, an initiative and even an organization. Studies of crises and disasters show that people perform well by jumping into the breach, yet organizations often get caught in "activity traps" or inaction. The committee chants "To be or not to be ..." while the individual picks up a sandbag and tries to keep water out of her home.

Today, with a highly educated workforce in the Western World, the rise of social science and the pervasiveness of pop psychology, we prize introspection. But introspection can be disabling.

The SOCKO™ system doesn't suggest what you should think about as much as it suggests *how you should decide what to think about* — and then how to proceed.

The SOCKO™ system teaches you to keep the most important ideas you have, and the most important aspects of those ideas, percolating to the surface. SOCKOs™ keep you out of the weeds and the minutiae.

SOCKO™ is a Management System

Twenty percent of most executives' time is spent trying to find things. Documents, phone numbers, contracts and letters seem to elude even the most senior people.

The SOCKO™ system allows you to focus on what's important and gives you the confidence to act, to go ahead and "Do It." Everyone can talk about a project. Everyone wants input. Most people can tell you how to do it better. But very few can actually do the project — warts and all. The great is the enemy of the good. Better to do something good than wait for greatness that never materializes. Better to *do* the project than just talk about it.

Sure, the "S" in SOCKO™ stands for Strategic. But the SOCKO™ system is as much tactical as strategic. The word "strategic" appears first to reinforce the need for thought. But the rest of the acronym implies action and impact. Do It!

At the same time, the SOCKO™ system ensures that the actions you take are useful; that you don't "Do It" for the sake of being seen to be doing it.

Some monkeys, when in captivity, will reach through the bars of their cage to grab nuts to eat. The grabbing makes their fists too big to fit back through the bars. They persist, but don't get to eat.

There are times when humans display similar behaviour. We stick with the comfortable, even if the comfortable is counterproductive or even destructive. We go to the familiar, even if it's painful.

Actions such as these have been described as "activity traps." Victims who have lost their homes in earthquakes have been seen picking up empty soft drink cans with unswerving concentration and dedication. This may be good therapy if you've just been through an earthquake, but it's not good management.

SOCKO™ is a Way of Talking

I remember a story from the Watergate era. Millions of people around the world were shocked by transcripts of President Nixon's language in the tapes from the Oval Office.

They were shocked not only by the profanity and evidence of obstruction of justice but also at how inarticulate the leader of the free world and his top aides "sounded" on paper. The word "sounded" is in quotation marks because although the words were on paper, we all heard them in our "minds' ears" as we read. We read "ums" and "ahs" and saw incoherent sentence fragments that never went anywhere.

Unfortunately, this is quite usual. I heard of a big city mayor during the Watergate era who decided to tape his morning briefings to see how he and his aides sounded on paper. The results were just as bad. He was aghast when he read what looked like similar incoherence.

The fact is we all, at times, finish our sentences with gestures and interrupt others before they can complete theirs. We also assume certain things about those who send and those who receive messages. We assume the sender has accomplished his or her goals merely by speaking them. We assume the receiver has the background knowledge to understand the new aspect or dimension that the sender is speaking about. We make assumptions based on age, gender, race and other matters. We cut ourselves off from learning, input, help and profits.

With the SOCKO™ system, you don't assume anything. Through repetition, clarity, simplicity, brevity and other techniques, you get your message through. By requiring that those who make presentations to you have SOCKOs™, you can examine the merits of the argument or intent of the question as opposed to the superficial qualities of the speaker. "What's your SOCKO™?" has become a popular chant among countless senior people all over the world.

SOCKO™ is a Two-Way Communication System

All human communication is essentially comprised of metaphor and metonymy. Metaphor involves the symbolic meaning we give statements, events and things.

Political debates in elections are not designed to resolve public policy issues. One of the major foreign policy issues debated in the historic Kennedy-Nixon television debate of 1960 was the fate of Quemoy and Matsu, two small islands off the coast of China. They had been fortified by Chinese Nationalists and were being shelled by communist forces from the mainland. Few remember that issue, but they do seem to remember that Kennedy looked better than Nixon and generated more media interest. The debate itself became a metaphor for how well the leaders would handle unforeseen issues in the future.

There are footnotes to those debates that I find interesting. First, those who heard them on radio thought Nixon won and he was mobbed and kissed at airports the next day. Those who say they were decisive in the Kennedy win forget their history. It was the closest election in American history to that date, and it's really only in retrospect that analysts said it was a knockout for Kennedy. Part of my post-graduate research involved viewing tapes of the debates in New York's Museum of Broadcasting. I found it hard to be objective after decades of "spin" about the event. If I hadn't known the result and the eventual fate of the candidates, I might have read more into Kennedy's furtive glances, shaking hands and spittle foaming at the corners of his mouth. Frankly, he looked nervous and unsure of himself. But, research in risk communication and perception shows that the old adage, that perception is reality, has a lot of truth to it. The Kennedy SOCKO™, then and now, is simply "I'm a winner."

Everyone is busy these days. The busier we get, the more time we spend telling others how busy we are.

Metonymy is a type of metaphor involving "a part for the whole." A good example is "all hands on deck." Everyone knows that it's the whole sailor, not just his or her hands who is needed. Often the characteristics of one aspect of a person, organization or policy are attributed to the whole. Classic studies show that airline passengers think that the airline with the cleanest lunch tray is the safest. That very small part of a complex operation that the passenger can actually see represents something larger and more important. After all, what else does the passenger have to go on?

How you speak, how you run meetings, your organization's news releases and all other aspects of your communications activities serve as metaphors for you and your organization. The SOCKO™ system makes your messages mean more, in more ways than one.

SOCKO™ is a Time Management System

Everyone is busy these days. The busier we get, the more time we spend telling others how busy we are.

Change has always been with us. Herodotus was the first to point out that we can't put our foot in the same stream twice. The person, the situation and the outcome are always changing.

But even change has changed. Alvin Tofler defines time as the intervals between which things happen. Most people believe that these intervals are becoming shorter and shorter. With this change comes a necessary change in our approaches to management. Daryl R. Conner says that "What has changed about change is its magnitude, the approach it requires, the increasing seriousness of its implications, and the diminishing shelf life of the effectiveness of our responses to it."

During World War II, Prime Minister Churchill and President Roosevelt wrote letters to each other. By the time these letters arrived, they were days old. In the early days of the Vietnam war, television reporters first had to get their filmed reports to Hong Kong for satellite transmission to North America. The news reports that aired in our living rooms were generally about 18 hours old. Now if the report isn't live while the event is happening, it's an historical documentary.

In business life, the fax machine drastically reduced the time available to business executives and others to make decisions. Then voice mail added tension and emotion to instant communication. Now e-mail reduces the response time to a few clicks. You'd better make good decisions.

Many people who feel victimized by voice mail, e-mail, couriers, GPS and blackberries are looking at form instead of meaning. That technological form seems intimidating, but the meaning is decades old. Forty years ago in London, England, there were up to seven mail deliveries per day. I doubt that any executives had an assistant ring a bell and halt other business each time the mail arrived. Yet many modern executives do just that today by having their computers ring a bell when an e-mail or deadline arrives. Much of the lack of time and concentration we experience is a self-inflicted wound.

The SOCKO™ system is the basis for an active, rapid and effective management system that recognizes that "fast relief" needs to be faster now. In addition to saying "Do It," the SOCKO™ system says "Get On With It!"

SOCKO™ is a Meeting Management System

We've all been in meetings, not knowing why we're there. The meeting appears to be an end in itself with little thought given to an outcome.

I know of a company that used to hold day-long Executive Committee meetings every Wednesday. That was bad enough, but then food would be brought in and the meetings would stretch into the evening. Often these meetings lasted for 13 hours or more.

The next day, company executives would meet with middle managers and senior staff to brief them on the Wednesday meeting and discuss follow-up options to be considered at the next Executive Committee meeting.

In an effort to streamline this process, key Executive Committee members began to hold preparatory meetings on Tuesdays. So now the schedule for senior management was: pre-meetings for half of Tuesdays, Executive Committee all day Wednesday and follow-up meetings for half of Thursday.

I wanted to know who was actually running the company? How many senior managers can afford to pull themselves out of the management game for two days a week, every week?

Another client has a beautiful boardroom with a large table. Twenty chairs ring the table. Thirty or so more chairs ring the perimeter of the room. I once asked the purpose of all the chairs. I was told that researchers, analysts, assistants and others attended meetings in case the senior people briefing the most senior people needed facts or clarification on the spur of the moment. I said, and still believe, that these chairs are really about status. You're not really anybody in the organization unless you have to be "on call" to brief senior people. You're not needed, but you'd lose face by not being present and then telling your colleagues what a challenge it is to be prepared for these briefings.

What if there were fewer meetings? What if fewer people attended the remaining meetings? What if those meetings were shorter? That's what the SOCKO™ system advocates and helps you achieve.

In addition to my formal academic work, I've undertaken some professional development and training at Harvard University. One course involved about 100 hours of "Leadership" training. One case study they gave us involved an airline I won't name to maintain their privacy. They had morale and other problems until a new CEO took over. He immediately set out to meet the troops. They'd find him in the baggage area in Tokyo, at reservations in New York and in the lounge in London. Morale improved. The CEO was to be complimented. This appeared to be Harvard's example of modern leadership. My opinion? I told the class that if I'd been the chair of the airline, I would have at least considered firing the CEO for not running the airline.

If modern leadership and management boils down to mock-egalitarian gestures and photo opportunities at seven figures per CEO, you can have it. In fact, when I returned from Harvard I had to deal with a high-tech CEO who needed to motivate his troops and deal with the media better. He was not good at these tasks and would not improve for some time. I found out that his skill was establishing and maintaining relationships

The SOCKO™ system helps you deal with the real issues in a more honest and productive way.

with clients. I looked the CEO in the eye and said "either get good at this or hire an actor to be a figurehead for the company." He shot back that the decision had already been made (that morning with me) and he was going to hire someone specifically for communication with employees and media and the candidate(s) had to go through my training before being hired. Isn't that more honest? Couldn't an airline hire a retired astronaut, as some have done, to be called Chair, COO, EVP or some other title to make speeches and deal with the press while the CEO runs the airline?

The SOCKO™ system helps you deal with the real issues in a more honest and productive way. In most rooms, organizations, memos and letters, there's a 300-pound elephant that no one wants to talk about. It might be race, gender, religion or the proper duties of a CEO. I say life is too short to pretend these issues don't exist.

SOCKO™ is a Speech Writing and Delivery System

I'm sure you can remember attending a speech or presentation that ended with nervous applause and audience members turning to each other to ask "Who was that?" and "What was her point?" Far too many speakers don't get a clear, memorable, powerful message out during a speech. Worse, many speakers actually can't be seen or heard by the audience and their visual aids don't make sense or can't be read from the back of the room.

Why does this happen? The most common reason is that most people are not used to standing up in front of a large group to make speeches. Don't think your skills in writing e-mail, faxes, memos or letters will be enough to help you prepare a good speech. They won't. Similarly, the interpersonal skills and body language that work well when you meet people one-on-one won't do much for you in front of a large audience.

The SOCKO™ system will shorten and strengthen your visual aids. It will shorten your speech, make it more visual and memorable and make you a more effective public communicator.

The SOCKO™ System is a Pre-Facto Crisis Management System

All the crisis and disaster literature is clear on the need to focus on outcomes, not causes. In other words, it really doesn't matter why you can't use your building. The reason could be terrorism, radon gas, a strike, a financial problem or a legal issue with the lease.

Your problem is you're out on the street. Your top priority is to find temporary office space or some other way of keeping your business going. So whatever the cause of the problem, what you say won't vary much, with the possible exception of terrorism or if the problem is self-inflicted.

In the event of an industrial or environmental accident, you'll be asked about health, safety and compliance programmes. The SOCKO™ system makes you codify your position on these and other matters right now, so you're prepared for any eventuality.

Take a look back at that iceberg diagram containing the SOCKO™ definition. Perhaps your three issues or topics appear too wordy now. They should be big picture items (health, safety, compliance), not statements, paragraphs or questions. The more generic they are, the more situations they will serve.

SOCKO™ is a Reputation Management Technique

Quite often I find participants in our training courses get stuck for something to say, particularly if we are dealing with technical issues. There's usually some resistance when I push participants to develop a message on health, safety or environmental policy. They're looking for more specific questions than I'm prepared to ask. I want it to be their responsibility to set the agenda, not the questioner's.

"What do you want me to say?" I'm often asked.

I reply that I want people to say the most important thing they can about an issue.

"Yes, but what's the scenario?" they ask.

I don't invent one, because I want people to be prepared for every eventuality and not just for the ones used in simulations.

"You don't understand," they tell me. "When you're under attack, you don't know anything!"

One course participant who told me this in exasperation was an oil company research scientist with a PhD. I asked him where he had earned his PhD — because if he could get one without knowing anything, then I wanted one too!

Of course, my point was that this scientist knew a great deal about wave action, physics, chemistry, response techniques and many other topics that would be quite relevant in a dozen different scenarios. His job was to get on with communicating his knowledge, not waiting for the perfect scenario before speaking.

In another training session with the same oil company, I got up, walked out of the room and removed a framed copy of the company's environmental policy from the wall. I handed it to an executive who had nothing to say and told him, "Say this!" I assume that's what environmental policies are for.

The point is, you need to prepare your defences long before your reputation comes under attack. The SOCKO™ system has you codify your values, beliefs and accomplishments in several key areas that enhance reputation. These statements and records of achievement are ready to go when you need them.

Even when you are involved in a court case, you can still protect your reputation. The widely held belief that you can't say anything because "it's before the courts" is simply not true. I have trained about 90 lawyers, worked with a dozen others, lectured at Bar associations and at advocacy training centres. I know you don't want to taint evidence or be seen to be arguing your case in public or through the media, and lawyers don't want to run afoul of their law societies. But that doesn't mean you can't say anything or don't know anything.

If you're in a lawsuit involving an industrial accident, you definitely don't want to talk about that incident. But you still comply with hundreds of regulations. You still have a loss/time record that you may be proud of. You still support your workers and encourage them to get rehabilitation as needed. You still support workers' families through counselling. In concert with your lawyer, you can and should continue to protect your public reputation regardless of what negotiations or deliberations are going on in private.

This is an unusual aspect of the SOCKO™ system, so let me give some practical examples from legal cases.

A libel lawyer asked me to help in a case involving a social service organization that suddenly discovered it was the subject of a newspaper "investigation". A journalist was making all kinds of unproven accusations against the organization, some of which were false. The libel lawyer, the organization's corporate counsel and I had a meeting with the executive to set strategy. We decided to sue for libel, get all the facts in order and use the situation as an opportunity to get out a good story to neighbours, legislators and other stakeholders.

The libel lawyer and I have had similar cases before and we know the first priority is always to get in touch with the journalist and try to put out the "fire" before the client suffers any further damage in print. We usually write a strongly worded letter to the journalist with a copy to his or her editors and legal counsel. The key elements are:

1)   Thanks for the interest in this organization.

2)   A recognition of the right of journalists to do investigative stories.

3)   An offer of several spokespeople to be interviewed to deal with the issues raised.

4) A suggestion of several storylines of public interest other than the one the journalist is pursuing.

5) A reference to accepted journalistic ethics regarding news gathering and the need for balance and fairness in reporting.

6) A warning that dissemination of unproven information and allegations will not be tolerated and may be actionable.

Most reporters say they wouldn't pay much attention to such a letter. However, the target of our letter is not the reporter but the editor, counsel and publisher. That's why we send several copies. Editors and lawyers are inherently conservative, and if they see a letter with legal and journalistic time bombs in it, they often caution the journalist. We want them to know that we know what the rules are.

In this particular case, we had drafted such a letter within hours. But weeks later it still hadn't been approved by the organization's lawyer. While the letter sat on his desk, the newspaper in question had no idea that its story was faulty, that its reporter had used incomplete and misleading information to prepare it and might well rely on the same information to prepare equally faulty follow-up articles. I kept asking the lawyer what was causing the delay.

First, he wanted to get all the facts straight, as I did. Next, he wanted to prepare a notice of motion in the libel case. Next, he wanted to file it and exercise proper professional courtesy with the lawyer for the newspaper. Finally I told the lawyer I couldn't understand why he didn't seem to want to protect his client!

That was strong language, I agree. However, the lawyer was focussed almost exclusively on a court case that would happen 18 months later, professional courtesy and detail. I was focussing on the next day's newspaper. We were both right but the SOCKO™ system and its use in the letter to the newspaper allowed us to pursue both goals simultaneously.

Another case involved witness preparation in Washington. It was a case against the U.S. government involving a controversial contract for services. There was a one-third overrun in the contract and I was trying to get the plaintiff's witnesses to tell me a compelling story in the form of a series of SOCKOs™. By mid-afternoon, after mock examination-in-chief and cross-examination several times, I still couldn't get them to tell me that story.

After several more attempts to get them to beef up their stories and be clear and specific with anecdotes and examples, one witness became exasperated. "We have all that!" he exclaimed.

When I pressed him to include "all that" in his responses, he showed me a triangle diagram with tasks detailed along its base, and, as the hypotenuse rose to the peak, it showed additional, unforeseen hours required to accomplish the tasks. "There it is!" he said triumphantly.

I asked if my bill to him were 30 percent higher than estimated, would he pay it if I sent him a similar diagram? I still had no idea why the contract was over budget. Was it incompetence, the weather or bad materials?

The organization's lawyer, who was in the room, had been trying to make this point with the client for 18 months. We agreed the case would be won by the best storyteller, perhaps supported by a graphic artist — and SOCKOs™ help tell stories.

My final legal story comes from a presentation I was making on crisis management. I was discussing the need for rapid, accurate dissemination of information when a lawyer interjected.

"You don't understand," he said. (I'm always intrigued by that introduction to a question!) He went on to relate a story of a client who called early one morning to say that his manufacturing plant had burned down. He'd written a press release and wanted the lawyer to review it.

The lawyer's response was that he wasn't in the business of vetting press releases. More importantly, he didn't want any press release issued because that, by itself, could be seen as an admission of liability.

The main thing that came to mind was the Monty Python dead parrot sketch.

"But the plant burned down," I said.

"It's no longer there."

"It's an ex-plant, in plant heaven, gone to meet its maker."

"There's a void where the plant used to be."

"Yes," the lawyer agreed.

"Well, I asked, "How does it create liability to confirm the patently, bloody obvious?"

I was being a bit facetious, but my point was that there's a huge difference between a press release that says "We're sorry we accidentally burned our plant down" and one that states "We're sorry our plant burned down for unknown reasons."

The release can also ask suppliers not to deliver materials, customers to show patience, employees not to show up, victims to go to shelters and so on.

Just imagine if hundreds of workers arrived for the early morning shift in freezing weather, only to find no plant there. That could be significant liability if it could be shown the company had known about the situation and had chosen not to inform its employees.

The SOCKO™ system codifies what you can and should say long before such an event.

The SOCKO™ system achieves brevity,
clarity and simplicity. It eliminates
the mush that most of us put in letters
and reports.

SOCKO™ is a Writing and Editing System

Everyone suffers from writer's block now and then. One way to break
out of this is to fill up a blank piece of paper with as many ideas as
possible as quickly as possible. It doesn't matter whether you call this
mind-mapping or brainstorming; it's a great starting point because we
are all better editors than writers. Getting something down on paper
and then sorting it out is much more productive than staring at a
blank sheet.

However, this approach can make your writing project resemble a bowl
of spaghetti. The SOCKO™ system can help you make sense of all your
data because it defines your priorities and points the way forward.

Stimulus response theory tells us that if you put your hand on a hot
burner, you'll move it quickly because of the sensation. You don't have
to wait for the brain to intellectually understand why you need to do
that.

In sports, there's something called muscle memory. If you perform an
activity often enough — say a tennis backhand or karate kick — your
response is instant because the muscles "know" what to do and don't
wait for the brain to tell them.

The SOCKO™ system can be stimulus response and muscle memory
for people and organizations.

The SOCKO™ system achieves brevity, clarity and simplicity. It eliminates
the mush that most of us put in letters and reports.

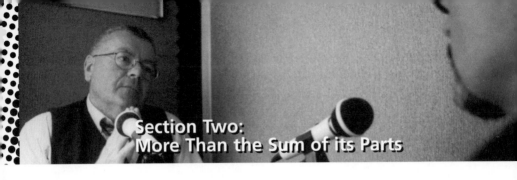

Adding to the tension of being a spokesperson is the confined quarters in many small radio stations.

The SOCKO™ system is your key to effective communication.
You may already have encountered, or heard of, "key messages," "aces," "press lines" or some other term used to describe a sentence or phrase containing the information you would like to be able to deliver to an audience. These days, many business organizations and public institutions also have "Mission Statements" and "Vision Statements" to define what it is they do and what their goals are.

While similar to SOCKOs™, there is one vital difference: SOCKOs™ are designed from the outset to have an impact — just as the acronym suggests.

A SOCKO™ derives its strength from its structure. The acronym stands for *Strategic Overriding Communications and Knowledge Objectives*. That may sound a bit cute, but please reserve your judgement for a little longer. After 15 years of using the term SOCKO™, I really can't think of a better way of expressing how to do and say the right thing.

Seven years of post-graduate research in North America and the U.K. into how people send and receive messages, especially under pressure, convinced me this is the right term. After helping about 15,000 clients with their communications problems, I *know* this is the right system.

As you will see, a SOCKO™ is greater than the sum of its parts. So, I'd like to start by analysing its elements.

Strategic
Far too little attention is given to strategic thinking in the communication process. Few people stop to think of the effect their words may have before they say them.

Did Bill Clinton really *think* before he said "I did not have sex with that woman"? Did George Bush fully consider the impact of his promise "No new taxes"? Did Alexander Haig stop to think of the implications of his words before he announced "I'm in control here" after President Reagan was shot? Obviously not — and yet the American White House is one place you'd think people would learn to think strategically before they speak.

The SOCKO™ system starts with strategic thinking.

Imagine there's a knock on your office door and a senior vice-president asks you to step outside and give a status report on Project X , Issue Y or File Z to a visiting VIP. You have a strategic decision to make. Do you reply, "Sorry, I'm too busy right now coping with Issue C or File D" — or do you step out into the hall and give that briefing?

Not surprisingly, most people assure me they would give the briefing.

But then I ask if they first excuse themselves and go to the washroom to rehearse what they are about to say in front of a mirror. Usually, they say they don't.

What about enlisting the help of a couple of colleagues to listen to the presentation and pose questions? If their colleagues are too busy, do they use a tape recorder or video camcorder to check their presentation for visual and audio impact? Invariably, the answer to all of these questions is, "No."

Of all the techniques available to sharpen, polish and hone a piece of oral communication, the vast majority of communicators ignore all of them, all of the time. And there's the problem.

The most effective way to make oral communication better is to speak it out loud.

However, most people have a resistance to doing this — even in our courses!

Now let's consider what happens when you get a request from your boss to prepare a memo listing the salient points of Project X, Issue Y or File Z.

If you write it out in longhand, do you read it over before handing it over to a secretary for word processing? If you do your own keyboarding, do you carefully consider your words on the computer screen and make some changes? Do you then review a printed draft? Do you make changes and corrections? Before you sign, do you ask a colleague to look over the memo to see if there's anything that needs to be altered? Do you put it in a desk drawer to wait until after lunch before signing? Do you occasionally let it wait until the next day and even discuss some aspects with your spouse over dinner? Of course you do, that's only common sense.

Now you can see the root of the problem.

People treat the written word with great care, reverence and attention. You probably use dictionaries, spell checkers and editors routinely to polish, sharpen and hone your written communications because that is what you have been trained to do.

But what about speech? If you treated the spoken word with only 50 percent of the care, reverence and attention with which you treat the written word, you wouldn't have a problem — and I wouldn't have as much business.

Overriding
The average human ear connected to the average human brain takes in just 35 percent of what it hears. The amount remembered after one week is just 10 percent.

Married people especially know what I'm talking about! Even under the best of circumstances, two people who love each other and care about each other can have communication difficulties.

I can assure you that most of the people with whom you will come into contact during a risk, crisis or disaster situation will not love you and won't make much of an effort to understand you!

They'll have difficulty hearing your message because when the tension goes up, "ear lids" come down. You have to make a special effort to get people to listen to you and understand what you're saying.

The first thing you must do is identify and gather all the various messages you intend to deliver. Write them down. Then try to visualize this blob of information you have gathered to be in the shape of an iceberg like the one provided.

The next thing you must do is build a strong, protective mental wall around that information for you to stay behind. Of course, you will be enticed out — to be negative, speculative or to speak about matters beyond your knowledge. The goofs, gaffes and blunders that people make when they stray out of bounds, or don't think before they speak, are quite astounding.

The most damaging thing your critics can do to you is to faithfully record what you say, add quotation marks and print it beside your name. They don't have to twist things or take them out of context. They just have to print the damage you inflict on yourself.

So don't! Stay behind your wall. Talk about the things you know. Be safe.

In the security and intelligence field, my clients refer to "safe houses" where you can go to cool off, or debrief. SOCKOs™ are a mental, semantic and verbal safe house. They give you some breathing room.

I like to use the image of an iceberg to remind people that they should disseminate only the most important 10 to 15 percent of the blob of information they have gathered at any given time. This is like the tip of the iceberg. Then you can deliver the next most important 10 percent, the next, the next and so on for the duration of the interview, testimony or speech. This is the most effective way to work through and prioritize your brainstorming notes.

ISSUE:

SOCKO™:

DISCUSSION:

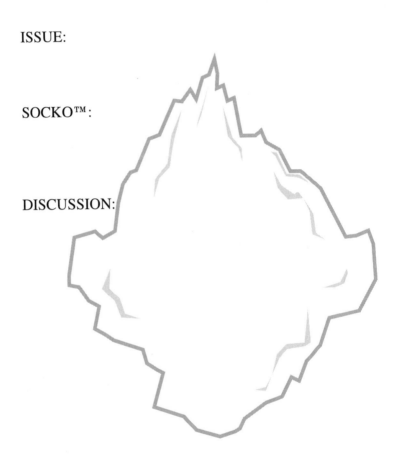

Figure 2: SOCKO™ Iceberg

The iceberg image works for me for several reasons. First, I did a lot of work in the offshore oil and gas industry, especially off the coast of Newfoundland. Some of the rigs are near where the Titanic went down and my clients have to build and operate rigs to deal with icebergs.

Also, the iceberg is a great metaphor for crisis managers. Most of the danger is unseen, but it is there. In the emergency response field, most of the remedies are unseen but they *must* be there.

In the communications function, most of the information you have at hand simply cannot be given out — there's just too much! You have to respond quickly and safely. Sometimes you have only a few seconds. The information you give out had better be pre-planned and safe. It should also be the most important thing you need to say, because you might not get a second chance.

This is why the iceberg works.

The most important 10 or 15 percent of what you know should always be percolating to the top of your mind. That's all that should be given out at one time. Then, just as real icebergs rotate, so will the blob of information in your mind — and another important 10 percent will then be above the surface. And another, and another.

You will always have at your disposal the most important thing you could possibly say.

And just as ice and water sometimes re-fuse, so will the elements of your message. You will find yourself repeating and reinforcing some aspects of that message. You will be close to achieving perpetual motion in communications! But the re-fusing infers that there's variety to your very similar messages, not rote memorization.

Imagine you are on a bus and a passenger says to you, "I notice from your briefcase that you're with XYZ Corporation. Didn't I read something bad about your company recently? What's going on?"

The concept of an iceberg of information may be simple but it accomplishes several important things.

But before you can respond, your questioner signals the driver that he wants to get off. You have 10 or perhaps 15 seconds to tell that person the most important things you know about your organization.

Should your questioner decide to get off at a later stop, you'll have an opportunity to reinforce your message by delivering the next most important 10 percent of your information, and so on.

In Hollywood, it's called your elevator pitch. You enter an elevator and press number 20 when someone else enters and presses number 10. Hey! It's a famous producer — and you have only a few seconds to pitch your movie idea before he gets off and vanishes. It had better be good. That's where the SOCKO™ system comes in.

The concept of an iceberg of information may be simple but it accomplishes several important things:

- It helps you to impart complicated or technical information in manageable bits. An audience that has no knowledge of you, your organization or its activities will have some hope of understanding you if you stick to the tip of the iceberg.

- It keeps you from getting exasperated or annoyed if you are asked the same question over and over again. Police, lawyers, reporters, regulators, legislators and others will ask you the same question repeatedly just to see if you have your facts straight. Stay focussed on your iceberg of positive information, and you won't be pushed into saying "I've already answered that once" or "Look, I've already told you ..." or something more combative.

- It prevents you from conceding something negative, unless you fully intend to. Many people blurt out "Maybe we should have done things differently ..." just to get away from the repeated questions on the same topic. But SOCKOs™ help you stay in control of your agenda.

- Finally, the iceberg allows you to take a finite amount of information and stretch it out for as long as you need to.

And you may need to speak for a fairly long time, without knowing much about the situation. During a crisis, controversy or disaster, I can guarantee that you will not have the answers to most of the questions you'll be asked.

Let's say a building blows up. You are going to be asked, "Was anybody killed? How did they die? How badly are people injured? Are you insured? Are you liable for third-party damages? How did it happen? What was the cause? How bad is the damage? Can the building be fixed? When do you expect to reopen for business?"

On the assumption that you are not a physician, lawyer, police officer, insurance adjuster and anti-terrorist specialist all rolled into one, the answer to all those questions must be, "I don't know."

But you can't walk out to face the cameras and microphones and say "Here's a list of all the things I don't know — and in my other pocket there's a longer list of things I don't know." You have to say something. So, you talk about strategies, attitudes, behaviour, goals, hopes, aspirations, capabilities and training.

The problem is that it's going to be extremely difficult to think of all these things during a crisis, controversy or disaster because you will have other priorities. You will be tired and possibly distraught. It may be 3 a.m. or 5:15 on a Friday afternoon (which seems to be when most organizations have crises and disasters).

And if it is difficult to formulate appropriate answers at the time of the crisis, imagine how preposterous it would be to do it a week (or a month) later. Obviously, the best time to prepare your answers is *right now*, while you are calm and able to set out your hopes, goals, policies, procedures and methodologies.

So, should the worst happen, and you find yourself facing a barrage of unanswerable questions, you can say, "It's too early for us to have all the answers. But these are the procedures and methodologies we are using to get those answers...."

Just remember "overriding" refers to the tip of the iceberg.

Communication
There is a vast difference between oral and written communication.

One of the biggest differences is the need for repetition. Repetition looks boring in print. Nobody wants to read the same phrase or sentence over and over again. We'd assume the writer was too lazy to edit his or her work. But in oral communication, repetition is not only desirable but mandatory if you want your message to be clearly understood and believed. To be credible, your message must be heard.

Another difference is simplicity. The ear is such an imperfect instrument, there isn't much point in exposing it to extremely complicated words and messages. The average university student has difficulty comprehending a sentence longer than 18 words. Keep it short and keep it simple. That means no commas, no parenthetical remarks, no subordinate clauses, no appositives.

Why would I be so concerned about the lowly comma? Commas are the enemy of clear oral communication. First, they often denote a list. There's not much wrong with short lists, but you should think about them, write about them and speak about them as if they were bullet points. A bullet point list has more impact on the page, in your voice and in the receiver's mind than commas.

Commas are also used to surround subordinate clauses. Consider the next sentence. "Joe, who is a jolly good fellow, just won the lottery." By the time the mind absorbs the fact that this sentence is about something interesting — winning the lottery — we may have forgotten who won, or that he is a jolly good fellow. The eye can go back and check, but often doesn't. The ear simply can't. The ear has one chance to get the whole message.

How about this construction? "Joe has just won the lottery! That's great, because Joe is a jolly good fellow."

This works better because each sentence has just one main idea. The second sentence also builds on the first and tells you how to think about the information (i.e., it's great).

The commas in the original sentence are also close to an appositive. The additional information within the commas tells us who Joe is, as much as his name does. More clearly the appositive construction might be "Joe, the jolly good fellow, has just won the lottery." Two sentences work better in many cases.

Parentheses are used too much by writers and speakers who don't know the alternatives. In the following sentence, the parentheses are used to fence off a subordinate clause, just as you would use commas: "Joe (the jolly good fellow) has just won the lottery." Listeners, however, have the same problem with parentheses as they do with comas.

Parentheses are also used to fence off an aside, the way a playwright would use stage directions or a soliloquy. Consider this construction. "Joe, the jolly good fellow, has just won the lottery (you know he's jolly from the look on his face)." However, the parentheses can't be heard if this is a speech and in print they slow down the reader.

I'd prefer to use a rhetorical question such as, "And how do we know Joe's a jolly good fellow? Well, it's because of the look on his face, which is charming." This gets to the point, involves the audience and keeps the narrative going.

While on the topic of oral versus written communication, let me make an analogy. We all know that visual aids help a presentation whether on paper or in the boardroom. Graphs, maps, charts and diagrams can increase retention by as much as 50 percent. But did you know that studies show the same is true for oral communication?

The key is to tell a story and paint a word picture. Don't be afraid to use trigger phrases such as "picture this; imagine the following; our vision is; what we see is; what I'd like you to see is." These phrases will trigger verbal visual aids as you speak. Think visually and increase the power of your oral communication.

Make sure you have these basic facts ready today. Tomorrow may be too late.

Knowledge

At a time of crisis, controversy or disaster, your questioners, critics and adversaries will not understand if you don't have basic factual information about your company or organization at your fingertips. The number of employees in the building at any given time, percentages of women and visible minorities, number of vehicles, annual sales, the number of annual fire drills — all of these provide a picture of the organization.

Make sure you have these basic facts ready today. Tomorrow may be too late.

Let's assume a reporter has been assigned to cover a routine event such as a political rally. While waiting for the event to begin, the reporter may well make a note about the weather, another about the people in the crowd, another about the decorations, and so on. At the time of making these notes, the reporter has no clear idea of where, or even if, this information will be included in the final story. It all depends on how the event proceeds.

Using the notes later, however, the reporter can write that the speech was "as flat as the helium balloons that fluttered to the ground" or the looks on the faces of the crowd were "as grey as the day" or perhaps that the politician's words "warmed up the crowd even more than the sun could that day."

Facts, data, statistics and colour are the staples of a reporter's diet and you should be prepared for that when you find yourself dealing with a crisis, controversy or disaster.

Timothy Crouse wrote a wonderful little book called *The Boys on The Bus* about how reporters cover U.S. presidential elections. It contains a line to the effect that, as far as the reporters are concerned, "a well-run bus is a well-run country." For reporters, a well-run bus is one that leaves on time, keeps to its schedule throughout the day with appropriate stops for work and refreshment and delivers them at day's end to the right hotel with the right baggage in the right rooms.

You might think that is a rather superficial way to assess a candidate's political worth. I know I did. So I took my concerns to Herbert Gans, a professor at Columbia University in New York, and author of *Deciding What's News*, the book that studies how journalists make their decisions.

I suggested to him that Crouse's book had exposed a major problem with the democratic process. I'll paraphrase his response:

"What else are reporters going to do?" Professor Gans replied. "They're young, they're keen, most of them aren't political scientists and they're put on a bus and told to produce stories. So you have to forgive them for covering what they see — the bus left on time, arrived on time, or got lost. Furthermore, if the candidate can't attract the right people to make a campaign bus run smoothly, how is that candidate going to attract the right people to run the country?"

In the minds of reporters, a well-run communications department means a well-run company or organization. If your news releases are effective, if your spokespeople are well prepared and can speak in "media-genic" terms then there is a good chance the whole company or organization will be considered efficient and well run.

You might ask, "What's this got to do with managing the relationship with shareholders, the public, regulators, neighbours and others?" Well, we're back to metaphor again. A well-run annual meeting is a well-run company. A well-written prospectus is an honest and well-run company. A well-run open house is a well-run company. These are all metaphors and metonymies. They are right in line with those studies showing that airline passengers believe the airline with the cleanest lunch tray is the safest. What other criterion do they have to use?

SOCKOs™ harness iconographic information stored in the recipient's mind. They serve as metaphors for what kind of person and organization you are. They have symbolic meaning.

Objective

By "objective" I don't mean unbiased, in the way some people think journalism should operate. After all, what editor would send a reporter to cover a case of child molestation or genocide and insist that she also cover the other side of the issue. There are some stories and issues that don't have two sides, they just require accurate coverage. In fact, most reporters don't even use the word objectivity — they prefer fairness and balance.

Younger reporters often take this a step further. They see themselves as David, armed only with a notebook, pencil or microphone, up against a Goliath company or government department with a huge staff, lots of money and unlimited resources. So they set out to achieve a balance by being overly suspicious or sceptical in their dealings with spokespeople. If you're not prepared for this edgy or even combative style, you're in for trouble.

In the SOCKO™ system, however, "objective" has a different meaning. It's the measurable, quantifiable, human, behavioural or tangible result that you want to achieve. When you are dealing with reporters, those objectives are headlines, leads, quotes, pictures, cutlines, subheads, sidebars, callouts, b-roll and clips. These are the elements that reporters use to convey a story:

Headlines   The big print that announces the story.

Subhead   An important wrinkle or aspect to the story.

Lead   The first sentence or paragraph of a story.

Quote   Your words in print, in quotation marks.

Pictures   The visual element in print or television.

Cutlines   The caption for a picture in a newspaper which appears right under the picture.

Sidebar   A parenthetical story providing background or context.

You must deliver your message in a format the audience can recognize and make use of. The less it is edited or modified, the better.

Callout   A few words of a print story isolated and enlarged to add punch or graphic appeal.

B-roll   Descriptive video footage used to illustrate a TV news item.

Clips   Also known as actuality, sound ups or sound bites (parts of interviews).

Quotes and clips are the elements over which you have the most influence because, after all, they are your words (or SOCKOs™). A recent academic study revealed that the average length of a clip on a television or radio news broadcast is about eight seconds. Public broadcasters and documentary producers may use longer clips; tabloid television and rock radio stations may use shorter clips. But the average is eight seconds, and that is not very long.

So as you frame your messages you must think in "media-genic" terms and you must be brief. Reference the frame diagram for a guideline. If you are not thinking in terms of quotes or headlines, your message will not be in a format that is useful to the reporter. The reporter is going to have to convert your message into a news format, and there's no guarantee your message will survive intact. This is also true for regulatory bodies, legislative committees, investigating officers and others. They will interpret your words and convert them into a format they can use and understand. Why not do that work for them?

You must deliver your message in a format the audience can recognize and make use of. The less it is edited or modified, the better.

Behavioural objectives in any forum can be seen and measured. What is your objective in a speech? Applause? Head nodding in the affirmative? What is your objective at an annual meeting? A show of hands to vote in the affirmative? What do you want people to do in your meetings? Take notes? Volunteer for tasks? Agree with you always?

The more you can visualize your objectives in real, human, behavioural terms, the more you will achieve them.

Sockos™ keep meetings shorter and more productive. Here, a group is using the visualization techniques outlined in this book.

Developing Your Message

Now that we have defined a SOCKO™ and given it form — an iceberg — it's time to give it some substance, to put some meat on its bones, so that you can begin to see how the SOCKO™ system can work for you and your organization.

Use the first iceberg diagram with the definition of a SOCKO™ to help you to think about your three most important issues. These are the issues you really want the world to know about you, your corporation, its policies, organization, hopes, goals and aspirations. They could also be the issues the world is dying to find out about you, whether you like it or not!

These topics or issues take the form of brief headings. Typical issues might be Funding, Compliance, Investor Confidence, Ethics, Health, Safety and so on. This is a perfect opportunity for you to take stock of what is really important to you and your organization.

The format to follow is: ISSUE — SOCKO™ — DISCUSSION. The issues are designed to do no more than trigger a stimulus response in your message delivery; they need to be general enough so that your SOCKO™ can address any number of specific questions concerning that issue.

ISSUE:

SOCKO™:

DISCUSSION:

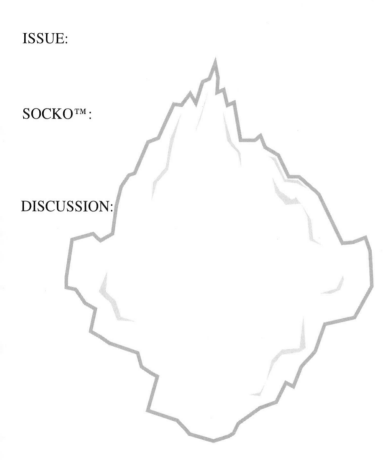

Figure 3: Issue/Socko™/Discussion

It doesn't matter if a question dealing with costs is phrased to ask if it is too expensive, or how you are going to pay for it, or even who will pay for it. Your cost ISSUE should contain a generic SOCKO™ that can respond to many of the questions that deal with cost. As the funnel diagram shows, one good SOCKO™ happens to address many questions that might be asked. That doesn't mean you need only one SOCKO™ — you need many. But it does mean that you get multiple use out of the SOCKOs™ you have.

Contrast the efficiency of the funnel concept with the endless preparation of Qs & As. Language theorist Noam Chomsky postulates that there are virtually infinite ways in which one can put words together to mean much the same thing. We don't have to have heard the exact sequence of words before to understand the meaning of a sentence. I take it from this that there are an endless number of ways to phrase questions and thus an endless set of answers to prepare. I'd rather make multiple use SOCKOs™ than start a Q & A project that, by definition, never ends.

MULTIPLE USE OF SOCKOs™

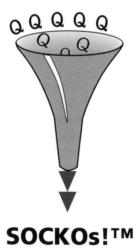

SOCKOs!™

Figure 4: New Funnel

Once you've identified your ISSUE, you should decide which is the most important 10 percent of the information about which you want to tell the world. This is your SOCKO™.

A great SOCKO™ just may be the answer to 50 questions you might be asked. But a Q & A sheet has only one answer per question. With SOCKOs™, you use versions of them over and over again. I say versions because you don't want to sound scripted. You will with Qs & As, but won't with SOCKOs™. Qs & As are like a "round" in music. The most famous round is probably "row, row, row your boat." Each person says the same thing, at the same time in the round, with the same notes, over and over again. It both sounds and is repetitive. A Bach "fugue," however, has several variations. The composer has some choice of when to come in, on what note and with what sequence of notes. It still has structure, but a fugue generates and sustains more interest than a round.

Once you've identified your ISSUE, you should decide which is the most important 10 percent of the information about which you want to tell the world. This is your SOCKO™.

After that you can add four or five supporting discussion points that can be used to expand your answer when you respond to follow-up questions. This way, you make sure you have enough material to present and defend your case, no matter how rigorous the interrogation.

It might help if you also think of your SOCKOs™ as the raw material of news.

People begin to pay attention when they hear the word "news" because they are expecting to hear something important or new. But what is news?

An American commission on freedom of the press after World War II came up with a definition which I'd like to paraphrase. News should identify fact as fact and opinion as opinion, provide full access to the day's intelligence and be a representative picture of the constituent groups in society. These are lofty ideals and we shouldn't be too surprised when they are not lived up to.

I like the definition of news provided by the late Phil Graham, of the Washington Post. He called news "The first rough draft of history." It may be important, have an impact on people and make a difference but it is being drafted on the run and so comes to us complete with errors, omissions, warts and foibles. Journalists watch the world rushing by at breakneck speed and then present us with a snapshot of the day's events and happenings. In that context, they don't do too badly at all.

Here's another definition I like. An old Australian editor once said that news is anything that causes people to exclaim "Oh......!" So, if what you are saying causes people to stop and take notice, it could also be printed in the paper and influence legislators or others.

That is what SOCKOs™ are designed to do.

Social scientists are very clear about the importance of framing and "signalling" oral messages, even though they can't tell us exactly how communication affects human behaviour. If they could, there would be only one brand of cola, one model of automobile and one type of cigarette. The others would have been advertised (or legislated) out of existence.

When it comes to oral messages, however, the academics stress the importance of **primacy, recency and frequency**. In other words, we are most likely to be impressed and influenced by what we hear first, last and most often.

You may also come across such terms as "compression" or "channelling." These simply mean using several different types of media to deliver the same message. The theory is that continued repetition of your message on radio, television, computer screens and in print will add to its power and impact.

The Sender/Receiver Dynamic

People seem to like communication models. That's why Marshall
McLuhan had a field day with "the medium is the message."

There's a simple lesson to take from his complex, sometimes impenetrable
writing, and that is that your means of communication — whether a
quill pen, a camcorder, the internet or a typewriter — will itself have
an impact on the message you make and how people interpret and
understand that message. A message of condolence left on voice mail
or sent by e-mail won't have the same effect as one contained in a hand-
written note or expressed face-to-face.

Some people like to equate communication with the transport of goods.
Many highschool geography texts have sections entitled "Transportation
and Communication." This is fine, as far as it goes, but we must not
confuse the two. A transportation hub with railroads, highways and
airports quite likely needs a post office, newspaper and radio station.
Certainly industry needs microwave, broadband, facsimile and so on.

The two topics, communication and transportation, are linked and always
have been. Canoe routes and cow paths got you somewhere, in part,
because you needed to talk to someone. In order to get there you might
have had to talk to someone to find out where the cow path was.

But there's a problem when people start thinking they are not only
linked, but virtually the same. This can be called the transportation
theory of communication.

Consider how transportation works. I set out in my canoe on a journey
and, with luck, I get through to my destination. I write a message on a
piece of paper and give it to a pony express rider or letter carrier and,
if there are no serious impediments, the message gets through.

But it might not. It is a hit and miss thing in the transportation business — and it has come to be accepted as part of the hazards of communicating. The point that most people miss, however, is that unlike transportation, communication is constant.

In transportation, you can choose not to go. You can choose not to send something. In communication, you don't have much choice. Silence is communication. A look or a gesture is communication. Not being in the room can be communication.

Remember — You can't turn off the taps in communication.

To communicate effectively, however, we need to examine the relationship between the "sender" and the "receiver." Too often, we expect too much of the people to whom we aim our messages.

If they can't or don't want to understand us, we usually blame them for not paying attention, or we fall back on that old cliché so beloved by governments, politicians and other power brokers, and blame it on "a breakdown in communications."

I believe the sender or communicator must assume a much greater share of the responsibility for ensuring the message gets through. An old adage used in education makes the point: "Start where the student is." Another warns bluntly, "Just because the teacher taught, doesn't mean the learner learned."

It is the communicator's responsibility to be understood, not the recipient's responsibility to understand.

We should remember that the receiver often has more to contribute to the relationship than the sender. If you're delivering an eight-second clip on television, making a two-minute interjection in a meeting or delivering a fifteen-minute formal speech, ask yourself who brings more to the table, you or your audience?

The power of your message is in the minds of your listeners.

Just think of all the education, experiences, thoughts and ideas already in the heads of your audience! They took a lifetime to acquire all this. How can you exceed that in the short time you have at your disposal? Sure, you may have a new perspective on a burning issue ready to deliver in the form of SOCKOs™, but you must pay some homage to the treasure chest of knowledge represented by your audience. In fact, you can get this knowledge to work for you.

First, you need SOCKOs™ to get and hold the audience's attention. Research indicates that you win your debate, or win over your audience, based on the weight of evidence or supporting material you can provide. Knockout punches are rare. It is the cumulative effect of your points that wins the day.

Then you can try to unlock the *images* of the events, memories and knowledge locked in the minds of your audience. Your listeners may not all be from the same company or industry group. But if they are all over a certain age, they will have some common memories of political, social or economic events. You can evoke those memories to get the audience to imagine, picture and think about the points you want to make.

If you need proof, listen to or read some of the great speeches of the last one hundred years or so. Most of the great speakers used images, stories, anecdotes and metaphors to convey ideas.

The power of your message is in the minds of your listeners.

Be advised, however, there could also be a negative side to evoking "stored" images.

We all have shared abstract concepts such as "mother," "needy," "home" and so on. Country and western music is built on those shared images!

But, thanks to the television age, we also share less pleasant images. If you are confronted by protestors at your plant gate and you inadvertently evoke stored images of police and security forces using clubs or pepper spray against demonstrators, you may trigger something you'll regret.

So make your message powerful and clear and get it out early and often and you will always be ahead of your adversaries.

If you need proof of how powerful these images can be, obtain some news footage of the Vietnam War from the 1960s or peace and environmental protests of later decades. I bet they'll tug on your heartstrings or get other emotions going.

Framing, Signalling and Amplification

Framing is important because it places your message in context.

If you don't care enough about your message to place it in context, don't be surprised if reporters (or others) choose the context for you. When people in the public eye complain that they have been misquoted in the media, what they usually mean is that their words have been taken out of context.

So set your own frame. Imagine anchoring yourself in the graphic frame in this book and be sure not to let anyone pull you out. You aren't in total control here because the people receiving your message may have their own frames, or modify yours based on *their* personal experiences. You may say the glass is half full while they are convinced it is half empty.

Social scientists tell us that the person or group that sets a valid frame first on any given issue has a tremendous advantage over those who try to do so later. It is very hard to "un-frame" a message, "un-spin" it, or put the genie back in the bottle or the toothpaste back in the tube. As one academic put it, "It's hard to un-scare people."

Parents know that going "Boo!" is the easy part, but consoling a scared toddler is tough.

So make your message powerful and clear and get it out early and often and you will always be ahead of your adversaries.

Framing is closely related to *signalling* and the *amplification* of messages.

GET YOUR MESSAGE ACROSS

Frame Your Message In Interesting Terms

☑ What is new and significant about my message?

☑ Does my message tie in with a current issue in the news?

☑ Is it a spin-off of a larger trend or event?

☑ Does it add an interesting wrinkle to a current event?

Figure 5: Get Your Message Across

Signalling is a kind of psychological wake-up call. We each receive tens of thousands of "messages" every day. An exaggeration? Perhaps. But just consider all the visual, auditory, linguistic, neurological, biochemical and other messages you receive while driving down the road listening to the radio. Go through your average day in your mind and count the number of messages received.

Messages have to compete to survive. You need to signal the listener that this piece of communication is worth listening to. Your message may then further signal that this issue or event is a harbinger of things to come. It's got "legs" and will be around for a while. That can be good or bad, depending on the issue and the side you're on, but that's how the system works.

Amplification helps explain how some minor issues can capture public, media, legislative or regulatory attention. This is a much more satisfying theory than assuming it's just the luck of the draw, or a slow news day, and people have nothing better to focus on.

Amplification allows you to build on, or reinforce, what people already know or believe. It helps explain how an issue moves between and among various players in society, such as lawyers, clergy, activists and others. The issue changes during this journey and your management of the issue must change also. I liken the journey that an issue takes through the various players in society to the path through a pinball machine that the steel ball takes. You have to guide the ball, play the flippers and be careful to not tilt the machine.

Amplification is also the reason that some messages "override" other messages. Terms such as "ecologist," "fisherman" or "aboriginal" had more resonance or amplification power than "oil company" did after the Exxon oil spill in Valdez, Alaska.

ISSUE AMPLIFICATION

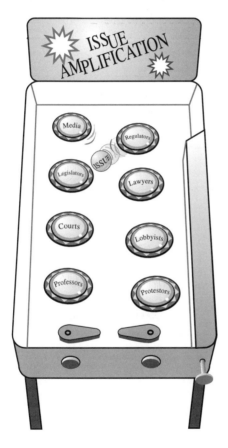

Figure 6: Issue Amplification — Pinball Machine

You need to construct your words and images to fight and win the battle against other powerful and competing messages.

So some words "trump" other words. Similarly, most images trump most words and some images trump other images. All of which is to say that the images of the endangered bald eagle, the dead otter and the oil-covered bird trumped all other concepts, messages and images in the Valdez oil spill.

Most of the technically competent engineers, scientists and others who worked for Exxon thought that the plain, unvarnished facts of the matter would win the day. Even though the facts were on their side, simple recitation of those facts didn't stand a chance against the images of the endangered eagle, the otter and the oiled birds.

You need to construct your words and images to fight and win the battle against other powerful and competing messages.

The Newspaper Model
Newspapers provide useful tips and hints for composing brief, effective messages.

One exercise I recommend is that you imagine you and your story appearing in a newspaper. It might just be your internal newsletter. It doesn't matter if you'd never be in a big city daily or even if you'd never deal with the media at all.

Look at the sample tear sheet of a newspaper in this book for 10 seconds or so and try to devise a headline. You can also imagine that you are making a speech or presentation to people inside your organization. Sitting on your shoulders (invisible to others) is somebody from the communications department who is covering this event for the in-house newspaper. Write the headline you would like to see this person use.

Why stop at the headline? Why not suggest a picture, chart or graph and suggest the text or cutline that accompanies it? If the picture shows two people shaking hands, you need more than "Joe Blow shakes hands with Harry Smith." You need something other than the obvious. Is Joe congratulating Harry? Is Joe being promoted or retired?

FOCUS AND CONDENSE

Figure 7: Tear Sheet Newspaper — Focus

Next, you can start on the story itself, but first you have to have a "lead" to capture the attention of your audience. The best way to find the lead is to jot down all the facts you have … the who, what, where, when, why and how of the story. These are the questions journalists ask, and if you review your list, you will find one of these facts catches your attention more than the others. This is your lead, your ice-berg tip, your SOCKO™.

Listen to news stories on radio, watch them on TV or read them in newspapers and you'll quickly be able to identify different types of leads.

Historic leads might begin at the beginning:

"This latest trade dispute really began 12 years ago when a backyard inventor couldn't get his lawn mower started."

The word "this" implies that a specific dispute will be the subject. "Latest" implies immediacy. "Really" signals you're getting the straight goods (unlike other stories to date). The "backyard inventor" angle suggests you're going to get an esoteric angle to this recurring story. No doubt the inventor brought something to market which affected trade relations with another country.

Umbrella or shotgun leads deal with the big picture:

"Workers in seven plants are affected by this latest trade dispute."

Rifle leads pick a specific aspect of the story to highlight:

"Ralph Smith thought he was on the right track when he took a job building lawn mowers, but a trade dispute has shattered that dream."

Some news organizations make their style books available to the public. These will give you many more examples of leads and other hints in preparing your messages.

The newsworthiness of an event or situation is usually judged by sifting the available information through a matrix of standard journalistic criteria such as timeliness, proximity, number of people affected, lasting importance, and so on.

If these elements are one axis on the matrix, the journalistic 5Ws and the H are the other. The attached diagram shows how this matrix can help you decide what's important. In one story, it might be the number of people and, in another, the one famous person. A large number of people might produce a shotgun or umbrella lead, and the same story, written from the perspective of one person, might yield a rifle lead.

AN ANALYSIS OF NEWSWORTHINESS

	Timeliness	Proximity	No. of People Affected	Lasting Importance	Geographical Dispersal
WHO will benefit?					
WHAT is being done?					
WHEN will this happen?					
WHERE did it happen?					
WHY now?					
HOW will it work?					

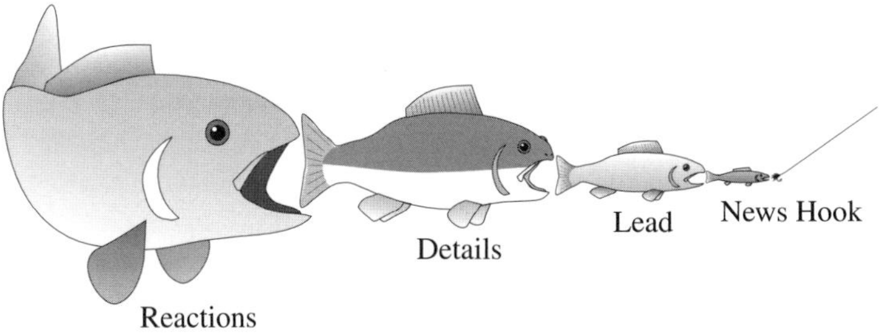

Reactions Details Lead News Hook

Figure 8: An Analysis of Newsworthiness

News is about people — the near, the now and the known:

The near   People are interested in what happens around them.

The now   Today has more impact than last week.

The known   People like to know things that build on, or amplify, what they already know.

This is the reason why relatively small tragedies or incidents in nearby, familiar surroundings often command more attention in our newspapers or broadcasts than wars, famines and disasters in far away countries.

Nevertheless, almost anything can make news. It can also make news in many different ways. Consider a minor, two-car fender-bender at an intersection in a mid-sized community that causes minimal damage and no injuries. On the surface, this wouldn't appear to have much news value.

But if one of the drivers was a clown in baggy pants with a red fright wig and ping-pong ball nose and the other was a uniformed policeman in a cruiser and the bystanders all stood around laughing, it could make a funny item — particularly on a quiet Sunday evening.

Generally speaking, timeliness is crucial when it comes to judging news value. But even a minor accident, like the one above, could be reported years afterwards if it suddenly came to light the drivers involved are today contesting a nasty, mud-slinging election campaign for high political office.

So go ahead. Make an arbitrary decision as to what is most important about the information you want to deliver, write your lead and compose your story.

Now just because I've spent some time discussing the mechanics of journalism, it doesn't mean these kinds of messages are to be used only when you come into contact with reporters. I use the newspaper example because we're all familiar with newspapers.

Even people who don't read newspapers have seen them displayed in vending machines and can see the way the front page is constructed. That's the way your speech, presentation or testimony should be constructed too.

Newspaper owners spend a lot of time and money studying how to capture people's attention, and keep it. I like to capitalize on other people's research!

You are now on your way to writing and speaking in the language the ear understands. Your message is more immediate, it's more interesting and it has more impact. But we still have a way to go. So hold on to your newspaper tear sheets, your headlines, stories and SOCKOs™ — we're going for a ride.

Freight Trains and Boxcars
If you've been thinking about a specific topic, chances are the salient points and aspects will already be in your mind.

If you've been thinking about that topic in terms of iceberg tips, headlines and so on, you should also be able to recognize the most important 10 percent or so of your information.

If you have already been writing and speaking those headlines and iceberg tips, you are getting to be a pretty safe and powerful communicator on that topic.

But please don't rush off and try out your new-found skills in an annual general meeting or courtroom just yet!

You already know the value of thinking and preparing your message before you speak. Now it's time to improve the message — to give it clarity and power — and we can do that by looking at it from different points of view.

Studies of how geniuses become geniuses show that they don't think any differently from the rest of us, but they *keep thinking about the same thing over and over again*. It takes about 10 years on one topic to get to the genius level, so don't expect to be there by the end of this book. We can, however, accelerate the process by revisiting your message from several different points of view. That's where the freight train comes in.

So return to your SOCKOs™ and pick your best short, sharp, memorable, honed, true and polished statement that you want the world to know about and write it in as brief a space as possible. Look at the drawing of a freight train and try to squeeze your SOCKO™ into the first boxcar.

If you think there isn't enough space, just remember that elevator in Hollywood and trying to explain your movie idea to a famous producer! A Broadway producer had his own way of testing people's clarity of thought. When stopped on the street by people wanting to pitch a deal, he'd hand them his business card and tell them to write on the back of it. Those who complained were told, "If you can't write your idea on the back of my card, you don't have a very clear idea."

So if you can't squeeze your SOCKO™ into the boxcar (or business card), it's not a SOCKO™. It may be a memo, a letter, an analysis or something else, but it's not a SOCKO™.

A FREIGHT TRAIN

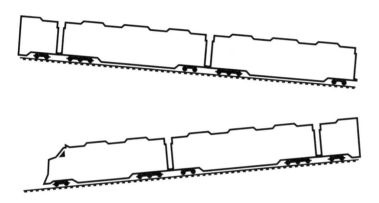

OF RESOURCES

Figure 9: Freight Train

Lack of brevity and clarity is one of the major problems we see in our clients.

In business and government these days many senior executives communicate mainly through written memos and reports transmitted by courier, fax machines and e-mail. They don't speak. When they do, they *sound* like written material that should have been sent by courier, fax machines and e-mail.

What we are often doing in our training courses is helping people relearn their verbal communication skills that have been allowed to deteriorate. We also see some of the same problems cropping up in our writing course. Computers and e-mail are changing traditionally accepted norms of writing and, more importantly, *how* we write.

If you can, think back to what it was like to use an old manual or electric typewriter. You had to think about what you were going to write *before* your fingers hit the keys. Otherwise, you had a lot of corrections to make and drafts to discard. It was much the same problem with pen and ink. And think how tough it must have been for monks to carefully transcribe rare manuscripts onto parchment.

With computers, we don't have to be so careful about the mechanics of writing because it is so easy to make corrections. We can spell-check, edit, format and print with a few clicks of the mouse.

I have always had to type quickly. I spent much of my life writing news reports, academic papers and business documents.

When I started using computers, it meant I didn't have to hit the carriage return on my typewriter. That made me a faster typist and so did spell and grammar checks (though these are not yet foolproof — they can't tell the difference among there, their, and they're). I don't have to spend precious minutes staring at a blank piece of paper trying to envisage exactly how it is going to look or what order the paragraphs go in, because I can take care of all that later.

Because of time pressures, many business executives will simply use the most convenient form letter or memo style of communication. The job gets done, but it won't be the most effective message for the situation. That would require more thought.

It is possible, however, to make this lack of formal thought before writing actually work to your advantage. As long as you don't have to worry about the mechanics of writing, you can think more freely about the information available and jot down an enormous amount of material. The SOCKOs™ or most important points will naturally percolate to the top during the editing process. Speaking, writing and thinking in SOCKOs™ becomes quicker and clearer.

Let me digress from the message for a moment to say something about your delivery system — you.

Not surprisingly, senior executives and business, political and social leaders have egos. This is fine in their own organizations, but when they try to "export" their importance to environments where they have no control, it can cause them major problems.

We often have to tell executives that while they may be Vice-President of the XYZ Corporation, they are not Vice-President of the legislative committee or regulatory body. To senior military officers we say, "You're not in the chain of command at the newspaper." We remind engineers and architects that it is matters of law that are being deliberated upon in court, not matters of engineering or architecture. We also have to remind lawyers that the rules of evidence they're used to in court may not apply on a radio talk show.

The people listening to or reading your message may not have your perspective. They may have a lesser or broader perspective, but there's a very good chance it won't be your perspective. You need to approach your message with a new set of ears and eyes. The SOCKO™ system helps you do just that.

This concern with male ego is rooted in the academic literature on "heuristics" or world views. The theory goes that big, strong men think that an accident can't happen to them because theirs is the biggest ship ever floated, they're engineers and they can handle anything. Tragically, some airline pilots about to crash didn't listen to warnings from subordinates because they were women and beneath them in the chain of command. In some cases, pilots don't understand what their instruments are telling them, and won't seek advice. In some of the so-called "men's" anecdotal literature, it is reported that soldiers in battle often die because they are too scared to tell anyone they are frightened.

Ego goes a long way to explain some of the great tragedies of our time —
the Exxon Valdez spill, Chernobyl, Three Mile Island, the Challenger
Explosion and some of the soccer crush incidents in the U.K.

Ego plays a role in smaller incidents too. The head of sales leaving
because he's been insulted, women leaving because they've been
harassed, customers leaving and trade deals falling apart may all be
partly because of ego.

I have benefited enormously from reading the men's literature and I
encourage others to as well. In short, inside each one of us is still the
little boy who didn't get picked for a team, or the little girl who didn't
get asked to dance — or worse. Those hurt little kids still drive a lot of
behaviour inside the adult bodies they now inhabit. If you need proof,
you can look around the local bar or listen to the local shock jock
on radio to see how many of us have really progressed beyond our
emotional teens into adulthood. It's important to constantly ask who
we're talking to and who is doing the talking inside us — the child or
the adult?

But let's get back to our freight train, where your best SOCKO™ from
the tip of the iceberg is now fitting snugly in the first boxcar.

Your message may be quite different from the one you started with. It
certainly should be briefer and probably clearer. But it still needs work.

You need another aspect of your message for the second boxcar. This
SOCKO™ (on the same topic) should be audience-centred. You may
have a great SOCKO™, one that has impact and meaning for you and
your colleagues. But if it doesn't mean anything to the average listener,
viewer or reader, it won't have any affect on them.

If you are dealing with the news media, your message must be aimed
at the homemaker, the cab driver, the nurse, the window cleaner — in
Australian lingo, "Neville Nobody," or in North America, "Joe Six-Pack."
That's who the legislator and regulator claim to be acting for as well.
It is imperative that you couch and phrase your message so that the
ordinary citizen will want to pay it some attention.

If you are going into a meeting of business or professional colleagues, you need to ask yourself what it is they need and want to know about the topic at hand.

It's the same with regulatory and legislative bodies. Research shows that these bodies are often tied into certain rulings or findings *before* they begin their deliberations. You don't want to find yourself unwittingly going against the current simply because you didn't bother to find out in which direction it was flowing.

This idea of simplifying messages is one of the most controversial pieces of advice I give. And I get an argument about this once or twice a week. The main objection is that I am helping to "dumb" everything down. I point out that I just want oral messages to be understandable to the human ear. The ear is an imperfect instrument which can take in only so much — even if you are a genius. I also point out that Freud, Marx, Mao, Galbraith and others were quite lucid writers, but many who write about them are quite impenetrable. Just because an idea is new, interesting or complex doesn't mean your explanation of it needs to be incoherent. There is more grace and dignity in simplicity.

I also get objections from professionals. I have the pleasure of helping excellent lawyers, doctors, dentists, engineers, city planners and architects. Many worry about sounding too simplistic to their professional group at an annual meeting or other event. After testing that concern, we've determined that many of the organizations' members are not familiar with a current trend or issue and do need it explained simply. We have also become convinced that professional ears are as imperfect as any and simplicity, brevity, clarity and repetition doesn't hurt.

Other concerns come from the college and university community. Academics are very worried about getting mocked by their colleagues for simplifying a concept in a speech, as an expert witness or in the media. They try to hold themselves to the same standards that they would for a peer-reviewed journal article. I tell them that research which cannot be explained to the average person is of limited use. If nothing else, we should be able to mount an argument that knowledge for its own sake has value. Knowing the facts of the matter either improves or illuminates the human condition. I am offended when people say, "It's an academic point" when they mean a "moot" or useless point. Saying something is an academic point should mean it has been thoroughly researched, reviewed by an independent group of peer academics and is something of considerable value. If more academics explained the purpose and implications of their research, they might have a better reputation.

Academic administrators have a variation on this concern. Many feel that their speeches to the Board of Trade, presentations to legislatures and media interviews have to mimic the language that professors use in their institutions. Little could be further from the truth. Even if the professors do kid presidents about outside presentations, the professors have to understand that the university has a reputation to manage and protect, and trying to imitate the language from an academic journal article will not achieve that end. In fact, it is important for all to understand that different types of communication — peer-reviewed literature, testimony, speeches, submissions to legislatures, editorial board meetings, talk radio interviews, television newscasts and many others — all have strict rules of presentation, usage, evidence, body language and so on. It is inappropriate to assume one set of rules can, let alone should, be used in other venues.

However, it's time to get back on track. The third boxcar is reserved for another important aspect of your message.

This is where you spell out the real, human, tangible, behavioural, memorable, quantifiable manifestation of your hopes, goals and aspirations.

What is it that you want your audience to do, say or think as a result of listening to your message? This is vitally important.

Consider a government budget. This is a complex document, several inches thick and very complex. I joke that it's so boring they have to lock people up to read it. In fact, that's what it's called, "the budget lock-up"!

When, after several hours of analysing and digesting, journalists, lobbyists and non-governmental organizations are allowed out to comment on the implications of the various measures, what do they talk about? They talk about taxes — the price of gasoline, alcohol and tobacco. Those are the real, human, tangible, behavioural, memorable, quantifiable manifestations of that government budget for real people watching the news at home or in their offices.

The chances are you are in the top one percent of the world's population in income, education, training, travel and awareness of government policies. Yet, if you are honest with yourself, you'll admit that these are the issues that also interest you.

At some point in your life you have asked, or been asked, did you top up with gas or go to the liquor store before the price went up? That's what concerns the nurse, the cop and the cab driver when the budget comes down and that's how you have to shape your SOCKOs™.

Over the years, I've had quite an education helping finance ministries, central banks and offshore financial institutions. I have come to respect the important issues that budgets or fiscal and monetary policies address. But it would be malpractice on my part to help an organization explain those complex issues while ignoring the simple ones that folks want to talk about on budget day.

Here's another example: a chemical company executive goes into a public meeting armed with graphs, charts, maps, diagrams and statistics to explain why so many parts-per-quadrillion of dioxins, or PAHs or VOCs in effluent or emissions are perfectly safe. However, he finds himself

Taken together, they constitute a powerful communications platform. They are your weapon and your body armour.

confronting a member of the audience expressing his fears of going bald because his father went bald after living for just two years beside a plant producing exactly the same product.

All the technical charts and statistics of the experts can't compete for impact with the image of the worried questioner's bald father because he is real, human, tangible and quantifiable. This really happened to a real person at a fixed point in time and space. His story has a credibility and a currency that statistics lack. That's why the third boxcar is so important.

You may find the picture of the bald father confronting the chemical company executive humorous, but, believe me, that's exactly what framing, signalling and risk amplification are all about. You will be confronted with memorable, tangible, human messages, and they will be more powerful than yours if you rely on statistics and charts.

Of course, not every SOCKO™ can be short, sharp, memorable, honed, true and polished and also audience-centred, real, human, tangible and so on. But your freight train of messages — perhaps 50 boxcars long — should have all of these elements, and others, scattered through it.

Taken together, they constitute a powerful communications platform. They are your weapon and your body armour.

Let me explain why I use the analogy of a freight train of boxcars. Yes, it keeps you on track and keeps you going in a straight line, but there is considerably more to it than that. To understand fully the power of the SOCKO™ system, you need to put some distance between yourself and the linear logic of print.

In print, the fact that C follows B and B follows A in a linear progression is often very important. In most documents, paragraph 8 won't make much sense if you haven't read paragraphs 5, 6 and 7.

The ear doesn't work like that. The ear is searching for connection, meaning and impact, not linear logic. So every SOCKO™ in its individual boxcar needs to stand on its own, make sense on its own and not be dependent on secondary clauses or parenthetical explanations. Each SOCKO™ must be complete and contain its own logic.

Another reason I like the freight train analogy is that it helps you cope with interruptions.

You may well be interrupted by reporters, judges, legislators or business colleagues but there's no need to become angry or flustered. After all, you may not be as fascinating as you think you are at that moment. The microphone may not be working, the judge or committee members may not have heard you or the note-taker may be distracted. They are entitled to ask you to repeat yourself.

In that case, just imagine that your message or SOCKOs™ has been decoupled from the rest of the train. You can repeat your message, or you can go to another boxcar and select another SOCKO™. It doesn't matter whether you work from the front of the train back, from the back of the train forwards or start in the middle. The ear doesn't mind, so there's no need to be upset that you're not delivering the messages in any particular order.

Because you are not locked in the linear logic of print you have much greater flexibility to select targets of opportunity and deliver your SOCKOs™ with maximum impact.

Guests on TV talk shows often find the host very close and the lights distracting. But practice lessens the nervousness.

Delivering Your Message

Carefully selecting and preparing your SOCKOs™ provides a solid basis for communicating effectively. However, there is a wealth of research material that shows the content alone is not enough to get people to really *listen* to your message. *How* you say something is often as important, and sometimes more important, than what you say.

We already know there is a great difference between written and oral communication. That's why it is so important to read your message aloud. You need to know whether it sounds right and whether you feel and look right saying it. You must practise and rehearse.

I recall once listening to a radio interview with the winner of an international public speaking competition in South Korea. Asked how many times she had practised her presentation, she admitted it had not been as much as the host might expect because she'd wanted to maintain a sense of spontaneity. She'd rehearsed only 18 to 20 times!

Now, that's someone I'd describe as a professional presenter!

I encourage you to take a trip to your nearest city hall or legislature, where reporters work every day. Watch the television journalists practise their stand-ups before they go in front of the cameras. Or visit a radio studio and watch a host rehearse her script.

Amateurs try to wing it. Professionals rehearse and practise out loud because the ear will catch things the eye misses.

Reading over your script or message is only proofreading and you are far too senior to be a proofreader (it pays only about $10.00 an hour). So promote yourself to spokesperson and rehearse your message over and over again.

Word Pictures

Another thing you can do to help make your message come alive is to draw it. That's right, draw it!

Visual images have impact. That's why television is such a powerful medium. The more we can get our listeners to visualize our message, the better we can communicate.

If I asked you to picture in your mind some ice cream, what would you picture — cones, bowls, bricks, sundaes, banana splits? They're all ice cream and there are many other varieties, shapes and sizes. So whatever you pictured is correct.

But no one pictures the Roman letters, I-C-E C-R-E-A-M. That's because we don't think in words; we think in word pictures, shapes, colours, patterns, smells and sounds. That's how the mind works.

If we are conversing in English and I say the words "ice cream" there is no way that you can assume I am thinking of a cone, bowl, brick or banana split. It's not your fault — the language I used wasn't specific enough.

Consider the fact that there really is no such thing as an unspecified thought. Just try to imagine unspecified ice cream. It's not chocolate, vanilla, strawberry or any other flavour. It's neither hot nor cold. It's not a big or a small scoop and it's not even a scoop, or a bowl or a cone. What do you have in your mind? It certainly isn't any kind of ice cream that I can picture.

Ironically, most words are quite unspecific, and we try to communicate specific ideas with them. But *word pictures* do evoke specific images in our minds. So, the communicator's difficult task is to use vague words to paint a specific picture in the recipient's mind.

Here's another example. Let's say I invite you to do some training at our country retreat. I tell you how to get there, what the agenda is and also mention there's some water on the property. What would you envision — a well, spring, pond, lake, slew or marsh? You can't be sure, because the term "water" is far too vague. What would you bring with you for the weekend? A fishing pole, bathing suit, pair of rubber boots or a boat?

The point is, the words we use to describe what we are talking about will dictate the behaviour of others. So choose your words carefully.

If you were asked to describe with your hands the width of a babbling brook you could be pretty sure that however much your stretched your arms, you would be fairly close. But what about a lazy creek, a rushing stream or a raging river? Each one is progressively wider, in most minds' eyes. And you wouldn't try to launch a canoe on a babbling brook or take a pair of rubber boots to a raging river.

The point is, the words we use to describe what we are talking about will dictate the behaviour of others. So choose your words carefully.

Speaking visually can help elicit certain behaviour from others. Wouldn't you be better prepared for your visit if I told you that my retreat contained:

1.   A swimming hole? or

2.   A fishing pond? or

3.   A muddy pasture?

The communicator's responsibility is to be understood and not to leave others trying to guess what the message means.

To give your message a visual impact, try to use the storyboard approach filmmakers use before they begin to shoot expensive film of very expensive movie stars.

Take a blank piece of paper and draw lines on it to divide it into six or eight squares. In each of these squares draw an icon or symbol representing an idea that you are trying to communicate. Don't use words or numbers, just icons. If the idea is justice, you can draw the scales of justice; money can be a bag of money or banknote; a decision can be a gavel and so on. The idea is for the icons and symbols to take you visually through your oral message.

You will quickly notice this exercise solves the ice cream problem. You have to specify the kind of ice cream you have in mind. It's the same with the water. It forces you to make decisions about your message and that makes it easier for you to say what you mean.

Now you "own" your message. You are not going to sound like a paid spokesperson mouthing somebody else's words because you've been ordered to by the boss.

Once you have rehearsed your message using your storyboard, you will find that you can deliver it just as easily working backwards as forwards. That's because the images you have drawn make sense to you *no matter which order you see them in*. If you write your message, or script, you can't start with the last sentence and read forwards. But if you transfer your message to visual symbols you can start in the middle, the end or anywhere else. It doesn't matter. You have freed yourself from linear logic.

The next thing to do is make your message three-dimensional. Your storyboard can easily become a cube with squares on the top, bottom and all sides. Behind each square, in the two-dimensional storyboard, are several other related squares with additional information. These are the sides and the top of the cube.

STORYBOARD CUBE

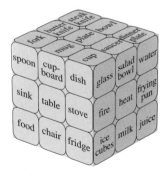

Figure 10: Cube

The diagram provided obviously deals with things found in a kitchen or involving eating. This is just a mundane example, but you can see how you might discuss the matters on the front of the cube in order: spoon, cupboard, dish, sink, table, stove and so on. If you want to linger on the concept of stove, or if you get a question about stoves, you have the related topics of fire, heat and frying pan behind the concept of stove. You can discuss things found in a stove (fire, as in wood stove) or on a stove (frying pan). You can also discuss characteristics of a stove (heat).

Each square is much the same as the tip of the iceberg. It's one of your important corporate values. You can discuss each tip of the iceberg, as the situation warrants.

When someone does ask you for more and you delve further into the topic, it's the equivalent of moving to your discussion points, to the next boxcar or allowing the next most important part of the iceberg to rotate and float to the surface.

Let's say your storyboard deals with corporate safety programmes. You might have a hard hat as one of your icons. On the side of the cube, behind the hard hat icon, might be a related icon, such as safety glasses. This might trigger a discussion of your eye safety programme, which allows workers to take safety equipment home on loan.

For example, "One worker who benefited from this programme was removing a motor mount from his car engine at home when the spring let go and hit him in the face. Luckily, he was wearing company glasses and his sight was saved" (a true story from one of our oil clients, by the way). You might also think to mention that 80 percent of lost-time accidents happen at home. A bar chart showing an 80/20 relationship might trigger that statistic.

The next icon might be a table and chairs which reminds you to speak about quality circles and/or health committees which promote safety. If your audience is getting bored or throws in another question at this point, you can return to the face of the cube and proceed in any order.

Consider the benefits of this cube of icons.

To use some military analogies, you can climb and dive, turn and bank, just as if you were flying a highly manoeuvrable fighter jet. This allows you to hit the target of opportunity that presents itself in that meeting, with that person, at that time, on that topic. You are intellectually flexible and mobile.

You are also allowing your mind to function in the way it was designed: as a random access computer. The human mind need not be bound by linear logic.

There's another benefit to drawing your message, and that involves the difference between analog and digital. To use a technical analogy, analog recording of my voice involves storing electronic impulses on magnetic tape. Some time later those impulses can be read by a magnetic head on a tape recorder, and sent down a wire to make a diaphragm vibrate. The end result sounds very much like my voice, but there is degeneration over time, over distance and with duplication.

Digital recording is a different process. My voice is transferred to binary codes to be retrieved at a later date. There is effectively no degeneration over time or distance or with duplication.

Words are analog and word pictures are digital. The U.S. Supreme Court has deliberated on whether one can burn the American flag. They probably wouldn't entertain a case involving the letters F-L-A-G written on a piece of paper. There is the real digital, actual flag, and there is also the analog representation of a flag (i.e., the letters on a piece of paper). The two are different and you and the courts react differently to them. (Just to complicate matters, the real, digital, actual flag is probably also analogous to, symbolic of, metonymy for and referential to country, duty, war, sacrifice, freedom and other matters.)

The artist Jasper Johns was on to this more than 40 years before the Supreme Court was. His representation of the instantly recognizable American flag, coloured with a waxy material on newsprint makes the viewer concentrate on whether she's reacting to an actual flag, the idea of a flag, the materials, or the artistic technique.

Similarly, you can't sit on a piece of paper with the word C-H-A-I-R written on it. The word and the paper are only analogous to a chair, not an actual chair. Consider how incomplete the communication is if I use only this word. If I ask my office manager to get me a new chair, there could be any number of things waiting for me the next time I arrive: an Obusforme, bentwood, a rocker, a stool and so on. I need digital communication. I need a word picture. If I say, "Please get me one of those high, leather, wingback, overstuffed, diamond-tufted, library chairs, the kind in which you might see Winston Churchill sit and puff on a cigar," I suggest I am more likely to get what I want. I might have to discuss colour, price and legs, but my digital communication has eliminated most of the chair styles that my officer manager might consider.

Most official communication from industry and government is analog. It probably means something in the mind of the spokesperson, but it does not translate into the minds of the recipients very well. Canada likes debating sovereignty issues. Everybody knows what sovereignty means. Yet ask an Aboriginal, an environmentalist, a Quebec nationalist and an Albertan what sovereignty means and it may cause you to stop using the word, because it's only an analog for what each speaker means, and they all mean different things. A law firm once bragged that they'd "exceeded their budget" this year. What they meant was that they'd set earning targets and exceeded them. To me, people who exceed their budgets spend more than they meant to because they're bad at handling money.

If you try to make your messages visual, they become concrete, digital, specific and meaningful. If you can't draw it, chances are you shouldn't be talking about it.

If you try to make your messages visual, they become concrete, digital, specific and meaningful. If you can't draw it, chances are you shouldn't be talking about it.

Staying Safe

All the cubes, icebergs and boxcars in the world won't prevent an audience member, judge or politician from asking whatever question she wishes. You need to plug in the most appropriate SOCKO™ available to you at that moment. But you might just be tempted to stray into new territory because, after all, you're doing so well.

Don't do it! That's how goofs, gaffs and blunders are made. The Venn diagram can keep you safe. You can see that the diagram (named after the mathematician) consists of a number of overlapping ellipses or ovals with a common base.

That base, where they all overlap, represents your safe ground. It's sometimes called the reduction or intersection.

This diagram reminds you to subject your message to several litmus tests. If the message doesn't meet all the criteria, you're heading into danger.

In oil refineries there's something called a catalytic cracker or "cat" cracker. The crude oil goes in, and out comes a range of petroleum products from "light ends" at the top (toluene, benzine) to asphalt at the bottom. There's very little waste. Your messages need to go through a cat cracker too. The messages will be refined, you'll be safer, and there'll be very little danger.

The Venn diagram reminds you to talk only about what you know *for sure*. Avoid turning hopes into certainties too quickly. Avoid what you wish were happening. Focus on certainties.

BE A GOOD COMMUNICATOR

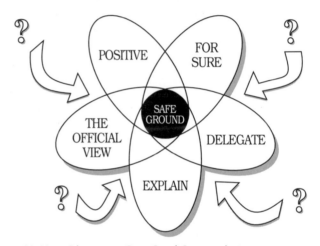

Figure 11: Venn Diagram — Be a Good Communicator

Speak about your *delegated* area of responsibility and if this isn't your area, redirect it towards the person who has that responsibility.

Offer a clear and lucid *explanation*. Don't be defensive or make a sales pitch. These will weaken your position. An explanation may not seem very compelling, but it has an aura of neutrality and that may be more credible.

Give the *official* view of this topic. You must be familiar with your organization's official view long before you find yourself speaking about it.

The last oval is a reminder to make your message *positive*. There's a formula I've developed after my research into the field of risk communication. It is that a negative is greater than a positive. This can be expressed as N>P. Negatives don't have to be proven and they are more easily remembered than positives. Negatives encourage more negatives. Avoid them at all costs.

You don't get any credit for who you are not and for things you are not doing. If you don't believe me, try going home one night and telling your spouse that you didn't stick up a gas station on the way, didn't smoke any dope at lunch and are not having an affair. You won't get much credit.

Negatives can be convoluted. What would you think if you heard someone say, "I will not say 'no,' ever." It's much easier to stick to what you will say. In fact, the universe is filled with all the things you aren't, are not doing and will not say, with the exception of those things which you are, are doing and will say. Stick to the shorter list of positives.

Negatives are often absolutes. The words "never," "none," "nothing," "nobody" mean there are no exceptions.

What if President Nixon had said, "I am honest" rather an "I am not a crook"? What if President Bush had said "I'm against taxes and want to reduce them whenever I can," instead of the absolute "No new taxes ... read my lips." When you use absolutes your critics only have to find one case where you didn't live up to your own stated absolute goal. Remember, never is a long, long time, always is very often, nothing is not much, none is not many (I'm joking). Absolutes have no exceptions. Avoid them if possible.

The rare cases where you may use an absolute or negative occur when anything less would be a problem and you are on rock-solid ground. If you represent a smokestack industry and a regulator asks, "Will this increase greenhouse gases?" You can respond, "No" — then add a SOCKO™ that you are committed to reducing *all* emissions, have already reduced them substantially and will continue to do so as fast as technology permits. Don't wait to have a positive dragged out of you or make the positive parenthetical.

If your message consists of what you know *for sure*, is about your *delegated area* of responsibility, provides a clear and lucid *explanation* as well as the *official view* and is positive in tone, you will be perfectly safe. But if you go beyond any one of these markers, you risk getting into trouble.

President Nixon's memorable comment "I am not a crook" met all the criteria of Venn except one. He was speaking about his delegated responsibility and about something he should have known for sure; it was the official view and it was a clear and lucid explanation.

But it wasn't positive, and many felt it also wasn't true.

That one missed criterion, and the focus on the negative, made that unfortunate statement memorable.

You can also look at the diagram as though it were a bird's eye view of the iceberg. The black area in the centre is the thick, firm, flat ice. The farther from the centre you stray, the more likely you are to slip off into the cold, dangerous sea.

Reputation

SOCKOs™ enhance reputations because they provide information and details that make people think better of you, your policy or your organization. That's why it is important for you to prepare them now. You need to have them ready and at your disposal for use anytime you have to respond to tough questions.

Never forget that your most valuable asset is your reputation. In fact, your reputation "equity" has a dollar value to you, your business or organization, just like brand equity in advertising. Protecting your reputation is as important as ensuring the standards of the materials that go into the goods or services provided.

The public affairs professional, crisis manager or risk mitigator should be creating reputation equity continuously to bolster her position in case of unexpected dangers in the future.

Reputation equity might be considered the difference between what the regulatory, legislative and communications environment might require of you (and perhaps has required of others in your situation) and what it actually does require of you.

It is not unusual to find court cases in which two companies convicted of similar offences under environmental legislation are subjected to wildly differing fines and penalties. Apart from the fact that judges have considerable leeway when it comes to assessing penalties, a big reason for these discrepancies is that one company may have displayed more due diligence than the other.

Invoking the so-called due diligence defence simply means that you or your company tried to do all you could to prevent the problem in the first place by means of training and emergency measures and then did as much as possible to limit damage. That seems fairly obvious but research in the United States has given us some additional insight into what judges are looking for.

The data show that a company may have had a poor programme in place, that not all its documentation was in order, that not all employees were trained and that the programme itself may not have been implemented properly. Still, these companies were given the benefit of the doubt by the judges.

In other words, you're better off having a poor and inefficient health, safety or environmental programme in place than not having one at all.

I think the lesson is clear. Companies and organizations with safety and preventative measures in place are bolstering their reputation equity. An incompetent training system might not do as much in real or perceived terms as a good one, but it does do something.

Enhancing personal or organizational reputation pays financial dividends in court and elsewhere.

Further evidence of the importance of reputation equity is seen in the insurance industry. There's an expression in the risk management business which says, "you have to fund the risk." In other words, the risk is going to cost you something, no matter what you do.

You can spread the risk over equal payments every month and if anything happens, your insurance company will handle it. That's traditional insurance.

Or you can put in sprinklers, take a safe driving course or do any number of things which might cause your insurance company to lower your monthly payments. However, those sprinklers and other measures cost money too. There's no free lunch.

Then there's "self-insurance." This is popular in the oil industry where some assets are so expensive, and the possibility of catastrophic failure so rare, that insurance premiums are very high, and sometimes even impossible to get. Self-insurance means you absorb the risk yourself and if something goes wrong, you have to make it right.

A more sophisticated and complex version of self-insurance sees a sum of money put aside to cover eventualities with the money earning interest when nothing happens. There can also be a sinking fund, which grows with interest and lessens with withdrawal for maintenance, that keeps the asset operational forever. Or, the sinking fund could be designed to disappear at the end of the life of the asset or after a project is over. My point is, reputation is just like risk. You have to manage it. Neglecting it has serious consequences. So long as you know what the risks are, quantify them and are prepared for them, you're engaged in proper reputation management.

Each and every one of us, every organization, enterprise and issue has a reputation that lies somewhere between the saintly Mother Teresa and Adolf Hitler. You need to know where you stand on this continuum. You also need to know where you are going because your reputation often isn't fixed. It is either ascending, descending or temporarily static.

You may not think of yourself as a public person, but you do have a reputation. You have a personal reputation with people you know, and a "hallway" or "street" reputation with people who have only a nodding acquaintance of you, your organization or industry in your town or neighbourhood.

A good person will have a better time managing a bad issue, such as sexual harassment, than a bad person will. That's because good people, with good reputations, can carry bad issues on their backs a little longer. However, a bad person with a poor reputation may not be able to carry even a good issue very far.

YOUR REPUTATION

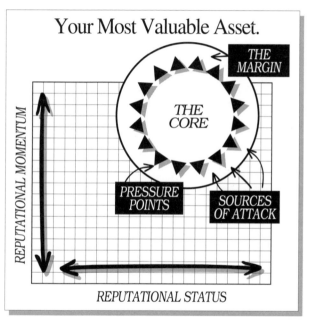

Figure 12: Your Reputation — Your Most Valuable Asset

In addition to your reputation, the issues you may have to speak about or manage have reputations. Drinking and driving, spousal abuse, marijuana and smoking — all have reputations as stand-alone issues. And these are also in a state of flux. Just think how we have changed our attitudes towards these issues during the past 50 years.

These are the core issues you want to protect at all costs.

If you know what the public thinks of issue X or activity Y, then you should be able to make a qualitative analysis of how these will affect your reputation. Judges and juries quantify reputations all the time in cases of libel and slander, patent and trademark infringement.

So, both your reputation *and* the reputation of the issue you are managing are important — and so is the reputation of the company or organization you represent. Before you can successfully manage an issue on behalf of your company, you need to assess and peg your reputation, the issue's reputation and the company's reputation. Then you can do the same for those opposing you. Now you are engaged in scientific reputation management.

So, you, your organization and your issue are somewhere on a continuum between Mother Teresa and Adolf Hitler. You are also going up, or down or are stalled. Pegging these points will let you know a bit more about how to act and what will be acceptable behaviour and positions.

Your reputation is made up of many things but at its core will be issues such as your *honesty, ethics, trustworthiness* and *efficiency.*

These are the core issues you want to protect at all costs.

On the margins are less important issues. Criticism of a company's casual Friday dress code, or its refusal to provide parking for staff, won't have too much affect on its core reputation.

The reason these distinctions are important to make is that many organizations, especially in times of crisis, wage battles about peripheral issues to the detriment of their core issues. This is another form of the "activity trap" we discussed in Section One.

Legend has it that President John F. Kennedy sometimes would complain bitterly to his press secretary, Pierre Salinger, about a story he'd just read in a newspaper. "They can't do this," he'd fume, and demand that Salinger write a letter to the editor of the offending newspaper, or perhaps an op-ed article to "straighten them out."

Salinger wouldn't argue; he didn't want to get caught in an activity trap. He just waited for Kennedy to cool down.

Invariably, Kennedy would raise the matter again in a few hours, or even days, and ask if Salinger had followed up on his complaint. "Not yet, Mr. President" would be the reply, to which Kennedy would say, "Well don't bother." It wasn't that important, and Salinger knew it.

This is what I like to call the Kenny Rogers' School of Crisis Management: "Know when to Hold Them and Know When to Fold Them." There's no point in getting involved in a big fight over something that isn't likely to affect your core reputation.

Another word or two about fights is relevant here. There's an Eastern proverb that says, "When you seek revenge, dig two graves." There's a dictum in the martial arts which states, "When a lion and a tiger fight, one is bound to be killed and the other badly injured." My advice is to try to avoid injury.

But back to the reputation management diagram that I developed with David Potts, the libel lawyer I have occasionally worked with. "Pressure Points" are areas where your reputation may be vulnerable to attack. Friday dress codes are not important, but hiring a catering service that requires waitresses to wear skimpy outfits is another matter. You need to continually examine where criticism might be valid and how it can hurt you.

You must reinforce your reputation in these areas to make you safer against attacks from your critics and adversaries.

"Sources of Attack" prompts you to identify who might benefit if you end up looking bad. Who wants to attack your issue, your company or you? I like Michael Corleone's strategy. The young Godfather said, "Keep your friends close, but your enemies closer."

A popular format with some television stations involves perching on high bar-type stools and fielding questions from the Internet, telephone callers and the host.

Now that you are able to use the SOCKO™ system to select, polish and sharpen your messages, and know the value of rehearsal, it's time to practise this knowledge.

SOCKOs™ are there to help you put your best communications foot forward. They will be especially helpful when you find yourself in a situation in which your critics, competitors or adversaries are putting on the pressure by shooting tough questions at you. At the same time, you need to make sure that your foot does indeed go forward and not in the direction of your mouth, where it can end up all too easily if you don't recognize the danger signs.

Q & A Pitfalls

The genesis of these pitfalls and their antidotes is in tens of thousands of interviews. I did a lot of interviews as a young broadcaster. But they were just the start of my education about how people ask questions and what types of answers work well. I learned a lot in the editing room where I had to listen to the interviews several times each, to check the length and flow. I also had to edit. When you edit, you listen for superfluous words. I heard how I sometimes didn't get an answer, or was satisfied with an answer to a question I hadn't asked. I heard how some guests could succeed and others fail with the same content.

Academic interviewing is different, but also taught me a lot. I have used the "life history" interview technique which developed out of the Chicago School of Sociology. I read transcripts of these interviews to pick quotes for academic writing. I learned how different the spoken word looks and feels. I was also constantly second-guessing whether a quote was representative of the person's views.

In short, I realized that people have a tendency to construct their language in similar ways when they want to attack you or your ideas. There are only so many ways to try to cut the ground out from under a person — and it helps if you can identify them:

The Set-up:

This is a false premise. It is usually couched in reasonable terms, but it is still false and must be dispelled politely and firmly. Don't nod your head to indicate you understand the question. Imagine the impact this nodding could have on your audience if the question is prefaced with a remark about the low regard in which you and your company are held because your products don't work! The judge, jury, panel or television audience could be forgiven for thinking there was validity in the criticism.

Q & A PITFALLS

The Pitfalls	The Solution
The Set-up	☑ Politely dispel the premise, don't nod.
Either/Or	☑ "Neither...the issue is..."
Irrelevance	☑ Dignify and bridge.
Sandbag/Blindside	☑ Key word, mirror or bridge.
Empty Chair/Absent Expert	☑ I don't know, I'll get back to you, here's what I do know.
Revisionist History or multiple question	☑ Cherry pick, bridge.
Flip-Flop	☑ Show consistent goal.
Oh, come on! Really?	☑ Turn up the energy. Reiterate and key word.
What if?	☑ Don't speculate. Tell them what you do know.
Challenging Silence	☑ Deliver another positive message, or smile and wait.
No Comment!	☑ Don't use. (Tell them why you can't.)
"Off The Record"	☑ Don't use.
Accusation/Negative	☑ Don't repeat.

Figure 13: Q & A Pitfalls

Another type of set-up question is designed to lull you into a false sense of security by asking you to confirm something fairly obvious. If that's all you do, you will quickly find yourself being challenged by a tough and unexpected follow-up question. The solution is to avoid simple yes/no, one or two word answers. Bolster your answer with an explanation and a SOCKO™. You may not always succeed in avoiding the follow-up, but you will blunt its impact.

The Either/Or Question:
If a questioner suggests you are either naive or being paid to lie, you won't achieve much by wasting time trying to figure out which it is. There is no reason for you to choose between unacceptable alternatives. The only answer to such a question is "Neither." Then clarify your role and move on to talk about your issues.

The Irrelevant Question:
A question can be irrelevant simply because the questioner isn't paying attention. Even judges can have other things on their minds when you appear before a court, tribunal or regulatory panel.

If you are asked a question that appears to have little or no connection to the issue at hand, try not to say, "Well, that's got nothing to do with me" while giving the impression that you're dealing with an ignoramus. Instead, suggest that while the question has some interest and value, you don't have the expertise to deal with it. Stay focussed on what you should be talking about.

Sandbag/Blindside:
This is a short, sharp, polished and honed ton of proverbial bricks that falls on your head when you least expect it.

Let's say you are having a rather difficult conversation with someone who suddenly glares at you, points a finger and challenges, "You're part of the problem here, aren't you!"

There's no need to panic, or get angry. You can use the same words to weaken the attack by responding, "Well the problem, as I see it, is …" and go back to your issue and agenda. We call this "key wording." Reporters, lawyers and professional inquisitors use it all the time to strengthen their questions. You can use it to bolster your answers.

It doesn't matter which variation presents itself, because your antidote is much the same.

You can also use a synonym of a key word. You can say, "The real issue here, as I see it, is. ..." In some ways this is better because "issue" sounds neutral, and "problem" sounds negative. You can also use an antonym to create a mirror image of the key word. Instead of talking about a problem, or an issue, you can point to a solution that you are working on. You have several options, or escape hatches. But you must stay on your toes.

The Empty Chair:
This technique comes from political debates and town hall meetings. Candidates or others who choose not to take part may sometimes be represented on stage by an empty chair bearing their name. They may be embarrassed and disparaged, and have no opportunity to defend themselves. This is what can happen to you if you are confronted with an expert you've never heard of, a report you've never seen or an issue you're unfamiliar with.

Remember the Venn diagram. Don't talk about things you shouldn't. You can offer to respond after you've studied the report and checked its findings. If you do not immediately admit your unfamiliarity with an issue, or situation, you may find yourself facing tougher and tougher questions about something you should not be discussing in the first place.

Revisionist History/Multiple Question:
This is a variation of the irrelevant question. This may take the form of a long, rambling look back at the last 50 years of a particular policy, how it evolved, and its current status. Sometimes questioners do this just to show off their knowledge. It could be a jumble of questions because the questioner is confused and stalling for time until she forms a lucid question. You may also get multiple questions from several people at once.

It doesn't matter which variation presents itself, because your antidote is much the same. Be selective. Cherry pick (see below) the aspect, the question or the person you want to deal with and respond appropriately. If you face another barrage, cherry pick a person or question again.

Flip-Flop:

An accusation of inconsistency: "Last year you outlined Policy X, this year you've changed it to Policy Y. Do you know what you're doing?"

The fact is policies change, because beliefs, facts and circumstances change. Try to show that in spite of changing realities, your goals, motives, hopes and aspirations remain consistent.

The Unfocussed Question:

Some people can't be bothered to form a coherent question and content themselves with casting doubt on your position and credibility by saying something like, "Oh come on! Really ... are you serious?"

It's designed to get your attention and throw you off stride. Meet it by increasing your own energy level, find a key word and restate your case: "Yes, really. That's what we're going to do and I know it'll work."

What If?:

This is a clear signal of a hypothetical question. Don't speculate. Be safe. Remember Venn. Discuss only what you know for sure.

Challenging Silence or Pregnant Pause:

This is an effective interrogation technique because most of us feel uncomfortable when confronted with silence in the middle of a discussion or interview and try to fill the gap. We put ourselves under pressure to say something, even though there may be no reason for us to fill the void. This is how we make gaffes.

Don't ramble on. Use a SOCKO™ to reinforce your position, or simply wait for the questioning to resume.

No Comment:

This is a bad Hollywood cliché that won't protect you from anything in real life. Basically, these words tell reporters and others that you have something to hide — and most people like a challenge, so they'll keep probing!

There may be several reasons for you not to discuss something in public. You may be ignorant of the issue; there could be judicial, medical, ethical and other reasons that prevent you from talking. Explain the reasons. Your audience may not like your reasons, but they'll be less likely to question your motives.

One of the main reasons people give for not speaking about an issue is that "It's before the courts." Most questioners will accept this, even though it's not a valid reason for not speaking. If you read the law society guidelines on this, and speak to lawyers, you'll find that you don't want to taint evidence or hold the administration of justice in disrepute and lawyers don't want to be seen to be arguing their cases in public. But, these rules still give you considerable latitude to discuss your policies and manage your reputation. You want to succeed in court, and in the court of public opinion!

Off the Record:
There's no consistent definition of what this term means. It's the same with "on background," "deep background" or "not for attribution." They can mean different things to different people in different parts of the world. If you don't want to be quoted on a particular issue, don't talk about it.

Don't accept assurances from reporters (or anyone else) that you will not be identified. If you don't want to be quoted on a particular issue, don't talk about it. You won't have any regrets if you abide by your own rules rather than relying on someone else's.

Accusation/Negative:
Remember that N is always greater than P(N>P). Negatives carry greater weight than positives, so steer clear of them. Don't write a letter to the editor saying, "Please be advised that we are not showing wanton disregard for scarce public funds at this organization and we don't want to see any more stories that we are." If you think this is a silly example, check your daily newspaper and you'll see it's done all the time.

By repeating the negative, you are simply bringing it to the attention of people who may not have read the story in the first place. So be positive.

Bridging the Gap Between Questions and Answers

There are many ways of responding to a question without having to blurt out something you'd rather not say.

I'm not suggesting that you avoid the question. In fact the "technique" you should use most often is a *Clear Question/Direct Answer*. This shows that you've done your homework and you know your subject.

BRIDGING THE GAP

Clear Question/ Direct Answer		Yes, because
Key Word		The problem is
Mirror		The opposite is true.
Bridge		Another approach is
Parallel Construction		My main concern is
Small Concession		It is also true that
Cherry Pick		The most important point you raise is
Refocus		The real issue is
Telescope		The big picture is
Microscope		One example is
Flagging		I want you to remember

Figure 14: Bridging the Gap

Problems and solutions are closely linked and the change of focus seems natural.

It is not enough, however, to simply answer "yes" or "no," "May 15th," "16 tons" or whatever. Add a SOCKO™. A question, no matter how simple or difficult, is still an opportunity for you to say something positive about yourself, your organization or your concerns and issues. Here are some other techniques to help you deal with tough questions:

Key Wording. This is a technique used by professional questioners. They will use one of your own words to move the discussion down a new track. You can do this too. Take a key word from the question and use it as a semantic bridge to get to what you want to talk about.

Mirroring. This is where you take the opposite approach. If the questioner wants to focus on problems, you can talk about solutions.

Problems and solutions are closely linked and the change of focus seems natural.

Another type of mirroring occurs in risk communication and simply involves repeating what the person has just said to you, or simply describing his state. This results in empathetic statements such as, "I can see you are angry," "I hear you saying you'd like more answers," and so on.

Parallel Construction. If the question is focussed on fees or cost, you may prefer to talk about results or value. Fees and results and cost and value are close enough in concept that they can be used in parallel.

When the issues or concepts are too far apart (e.g., the question is about fees but you wish to talk about the qualifications of those charging the fees) you will have to find a semantic bridge or use another technique to bring the concepts closer together.

Concessions should be very small and designed to help you make a larger point. A complaint about the service provided by your organization may cause a customer to exclaim, "I'm mad as hell and I'm not going to take it any more!"

Your response could be "I'm very sorry you feel that way. Regardless of what we may have done to make you mad, I hope you will let us put things right." This helps you display empathy without giving away the store and refocusses attention on your ability to make good.

It always amazes me how often service providers forget what a powerful tool a simple apology can be. Customer service is another application of the SOCKO™ system and involves timely responses, expressing empathy, asking the customer what you can do to correct the situation, then exceeding that request.

For example, if a neighbour complains that mud from your construction site splattered her car and is demanding it be washed, the best approach is to agree. But you can exceed the neighbour's expectations by also having the car waxed. In addition to restoring your status, this may isolate the complainant from other neighbours who may also be grumbling about your site.

Some speakers overdo concessions. Don't say "I see your point," if you don't want to be quoted as agreeing with the point. The concession might be "I understand you are frustrated and you've expressed your view well. I appreciate knowing your views and I hope to be able to help." Some use concessions to get off the topic. If you are being accused of doing something bad in the past, but you have no knowledge of it, don't say "Well, perhaps no one knew any better," just to get off the topic. That's how you'll be quoted and no one will see the other five times you said other things. You may also be paraphrased as "conceding that your organization does not have a history of knowing right from wrong." Concessions should be small and create a bridge to the questioner: "No one is perfect, but here's what we're trying to do now."

Cherry Picking. This is the solution to the bothersome multiple question from one individual or several people. Be selective and focus on one aspect about which you are knowledgeable and comfortable.

Example: "How can you explain this disaster? Why did it happen in your jurisdiction and what are you going to do about it?"

Solution: "We're going to ensure that people get to shelters quickly."
(Cherry pick; direct answer.)

Better: "We're trying to analyze those questions but our main focus right now is getting people into shelters." (Small concession, refocus.)

Better still: "No one knows all the answers but we may find out soon. We'll keep you posted, but for now we're focussing our attention on getting people into shelters." (Direct answer precluding a follow-up, small concession, refocus.)

Refocussing allows you to look at an issue from a different perspective. You don't have to accept the questioner's point of view. You can refocus from the point of view of the tall, the short, the rich, the poor, the north, south, east or west.

Example: "Why did you waste money on this ...?"

Solution: "My main focus right now is. ..."(Refocus, parallel construction.)

Better: "Finances are important but my main focus right now is. ..."(Concession, dignify, refocus.)

Better still: "Finances are important and we'll provide an accounting in due course, but right now we must stay focussed on. ..."

Telescoping shifts the focus to the big picture. Instead of talking about the needs of one community, you can stress the needs of a country or continent.

Example: "Why did you waste money on this ...?"

Solution: "Our overall financial picture is very strong."

Better: "We're not happy about this one area, but overall our financial picture is very strong." (Concession, telescope or refocus.)

Better still: "Not all of our decisions are perfect. However, the vast majority are excellent and that's why our overall financial picture is very strong." (Concession, telescope, bridge.)

Microscoping is the opposite. It shifts the focus to the smaller, more personal picture. One family's needs, for example, may be easier to understand than an entire population's.

Example: "Why did you waste money on this ...?"

Solution: "While not all of our decisions are perfect, the vast majority are excellent, which makes our overall financial picture sound. Look at what we've been done for our oldest victim. ..." (Concession, telescope, bridge and microscope.)

Flagging. This makes sure that you identify the issues or concerns that you want to focus on; they may be completely different from those in the mind of your questioner. If you don't "flag" them, they will be ignored in the discussion.

Example: "Why did you waste money on this ...?"

Solution: "Do you mind if we focus on the victims for a moment. ..."

Better: "I'd like to deal with that, but first I want to. ..."

Better still: "We'll have the answer to that in due course, but the most important thing right now is. ..."

These ten techniques may at first seem to be complicated and difficult to remember. Like most skills they will require practice. However, as you can see in the bridging, phrases don't have to be complicated at all. Here are some more:

Mirroring, Refocussing and Flagging
- The real issue here is ....
- I'd like to emphasize ....
- Let me begin with ....
- I'd like to focus on ....

Cherry Picking
- The most important point you raise is ....
- Our main concern now is ....
- Your question raises the important issue of ....
- Your question is important but right now we must focus on ....

Small Concessions
- Perhaps, but we're working on ....
- That may be part of the reason we are ....
- I understand your concerns ....
- I can see how someone might get that impression ....

Telescoping
- All our customers are treated with respect ....
- Everyone will benefit in several ways ....
- Our history in this area is ....

Microscoping
- One case where this did work was ....
- Ms. Bloggs benefited from this plan ....
- I was talking to one affected person who said ....

Remember: anything that allows you to move from the questioner's agenda to your own is "a bridge."

Answering Questions by Not Answering Them

Generally speaking, it is always better to answer questions than to avoid them. In some circumstances, however, there may be little choice. You may not have all the information, your knowledge may be incomplete or there may be legal or other restrictions. Even so, it is possible to not answer without damaging your credibility.

Here are some options (in ascending order of credibility).

1. Silence (ignore both the question and questioner)

2. Bypassing (a psychological term, meaning to play dumb)

Example: "Why did you waste money on this ...?"

Solution: "You know, we are really very careful with scarce public
             funds. ..."

Richard Nixon's favourite, "I'm glad you asked me that question," is
a version of bypassing. Nobody was under any illusions about how
glad he was.

3. Resistance

Example: "Why did you waste money on this ...?"

Solution: "I can't discuss that now."

Better: "I can't discuss that right now. It's before the courts."
             Or
             "I've only just arrived and I don't have all the facts."

4. Attack (negative resistance)

Example: "Why did you waste money on this ...?"

Solution: "That's not the question. You should be asking about the
             victims. I'm shocked you can be so shallow."

This is a high-risk approach. Few people can carry it off. Margaret Thatcher
did, because she had a reputation for being a tough and unsympathetic
person. One who used the technique to his detriment was the chairman
of Exxon at the time of the Valdez oil spill. Asked why he didn't have
enough oil dispersant available to deal with the spill, L.G. Rawl chose
to imply that the questioner wasn't really interested in seeing the oil

cleaned up.

Attacking the motives or highlighting the failings of a questioner is a transparent technique used by people who are unprepared, or badly prepared, to answer tough questions. It is no substitute for a positive answer outlining your policy, goals, or beliefs.

5.   Parallel response

Example: "Why did you waste money on this ...?"

Solution: "Victims need our attention the most right now ...."
              (Refocus from money to victims and hold out hope
              of an answer later.)

There are several other styles of response that would be equally effective depending on the question, questioner, answer, responder, venue and so on. By now it should be obvious that use of a phrase to dignify the question makes it easier to divert attention away from money and towards victims. The response will appear to be more directly related and so will have more impact.

Some examples:
•   "That's a good question...." (trite and obvious).
•   "There are a number of important questions we must deal with ...."
•   "Money is important, but not as important right now as the victims ...."
•   "We're working to get that answer ...."

You can also use key words to link the subject you don't want to discuss with one you do:

•   "The money we've freed up is going to help victims."
•   "We want to ensure no time is wasted in reaching and helping victims."
•   "The wise use of resources is important and I know we have adequate funds to help victims."

Safe Houses

SOCKOs™ offer safety when you face danger, just like safe houses offer shelter to spies.

Consider how we know something to be true. Perhaps we experienced it — we saw it, touched it, tasted it, heard it or smelled it. Some philosophers and psychologists believe that sensory perception was the beginning of language and shared experience. The first person to touch a fire may have exclaimed "Owe" or "Haa." That may have evolved to "hot" in English and "chaud" in French.

No one knows for sure, but after sensory perception humans might have strung together several shared sensations or neurological events into communication. Occasionally we can be deceived by our senses, but in general we believe them and trust them.

We may know someone else who saw it, touched it, etc., and then told us about it. The information is second-hand, but if we know and trust the person, their information may also be credible.

We may also believe an expert whom we've never met, but has great credentials. If we then use that information as part of our own case, we are engaging in "credibility transfer" — we hope the expert's credibility will rub off on us.

Conversely, if we use information from a source with low credibility, we risk experiencing "credibility reversal" — that's loss of credibility through association. This ignores the fact that a good person can have a bad idea and a bad person can have a good one, but we generally assess ideas, in part, based on the credibility of the source.

In some cases we recognize what we take to be an obvious truth, even though it is buried deep in the fog of argument or dispute. Take the logging industry for example. There is actually some scientific information that clear-cutting may be the most environmentally sound way to deal with some forests.

It is imperative that you don't respond
belligerently. Stay cool, be polite, treat the
question with dignity (even if it doesn't
deserve it) and, above all, be positive.

Hard to believe, but I've heard it. While that data can be the subject of
endless debate, what isn't open for debate is that a forest that has been
clear-cut is different from a forest that hasn't.

Even something as simple as the number of trees in my backyard might
be the subject of debate. You might count ten, miss one, and be wrong.
One tree might be dead. What you call a tree, I might call a large bush.

Anyone who has teenage children can imagine the endless debate that
could ensue. You might even argue whether there should be trees in a
backyard. Some people might not like the leaves, the shade or the effect
of the roots on the home's foundation.

What can't be debated, though, is that a backyard with trees is different
from a backyard without trees. All our senses and experience tell us
that, for good or ill, a backyard with no trees looks, feels, smells and is
quite different.

Statements which are not open to debate can be your "safe house."
They're a starting point for a discussion, about which there can be little
or no argument.

When you step out of your safe house to confront your critics, adversaries or competitors, you might still be attacked with tough questions.
Being criticized, whether directly or by implication, is never a pleasant
experience.

It is imperative that you don't respond belligerently. Stay
cool, be polite, treat the question with dignity (even if it
doesn't deserve it) and, above all, be positive.

What follows are examples of some of the pitfalls and traps listed above,
matched with techniques to help you deal with them. Notice that I
sometimes suggest using two techniques to deal with the same problem.
This is like a backhand in tennis where you use both hands for more
strength.

The Set-up:

Example: "Consider the low regard people have for this product anyway."

Solution: "I think what a lot of people agree on is that this product does the following ...." (Refocussing.)

The Either/Or Question:

Example: "Either you're naive or being paid to lie ...."

Solution: "Neither ...." (Direct answer.)

Better: "Neither, my main role is ...." (Direct answer and bridge.)

Better still: "My main role is ...." (Refocus and a parallel bridge.)

Even better: "Actually, my main accomplishment since joining this company has been ..." (Instead of attacking the questioner, refocus on your accomplishments. The term actually is a soft refocus.)

The Irrelevant Question:

Example: "Why are corn prices so high?"

Solution: "Our main work in agriculture is the production of tractor parts." (Parallel refocus.)

Better: "Corn prices are important to our business, but I don't have much information on that topic. My responsibility is in making tractor parts." (Dignify the question, delegate to others, refocus.)

Better still: "While corn prices are an important issue, my responsibility is in manufacturing tractor parts. However, I'm sure one of our economists would have some data on that and I'd be happy to refer you to her." (Dignify the question, harder delegation to others, refocus.)

Even Better: "We'd all like to know the answer to that because corn prices are an important factor in our business. We make tractor parts and our economists keep a close eye on agricultural prices. I'm sure they'll soon have some answers. When they do, I'll be happy to refer you to them. Meanwhile, I can tell you how our tractor parts help farmers keep their costs down." [Dignify the question, even harder delegation to others at a later date, refocus, bridge].

Don't get carried away! You don't want long answers, but the example above shows you the variety of techniques available.

Sandbag:

Example: "You're part of the problem ...."

Solution: "No I'm not ..." (Direct answer, but negative and confrontational.)

Better: "The problem as I see it is ...." (Key word, bridge.)

Better still: "The issue we're making progress on is ..." (Key concept, refocus, bridge.)

Even better: "The solution that's almost ready is ...." (Key concept, mirrored, bridge.)

The Empty Chair:

Example: "I have a copy of the Smith report which conclusively proves ..."

Solution: "I can't help you with that because I haven't seen it."

Better: "I haven't seen that report. I'd be happy to give you an opinion when I've read it. What I can tell you on that topic is ..." (Admission, which is a direct answer, offer, bridge.)

Better still:	"I haven't seen that report. I'm sure some of our researchers have and I'd be happy to refer you to them. What I can tell you is …" (Admission, stronger offer and rationale, bridge.)

Revisionist History/Multiple Question:

Example:	"How did this happen? Why did it happen? What are you going to do about the victims?"
Solution:	"We're setting up shelters for victims right now …." (Cherry pick one question.)
Better:	"We're working on some of those questions right now, but our most important goal is to get shelters set up for victims." (Dignify, direct answer, bridge.)

Flip-Flop:

Example:	"You said shelters were the most important goal. Now you say it's hiring insurance investigators. Why have you changed your mind?"
Solution:	"Our goal is always the welfare of victims. Now we find the best thing for them is getting their insurance claims settled." (Consistency, bridge.)

The Unfocussed Question:

Example:	"Oh come on! Really?"
Solution:	"Yes." (Direct answer.)
Better:	"Yes, really. That's what we're going to do and I know it'll work." (Direct answer, key word, bridge to efficacy.)

What If?

Example: "What if victims' claims are turned down?"

Solution: "The real issue here is getting those insurance people working." (Refocus, parallel bridge.)

Better: "We don't want anyone to suffer. We'll monitor those claims to see if the victims are getting the help they need. Right now we want to get the insurance people working." (Empathy, action, refocus.)

Challenging Silence or Pregnant Pause:

Solution: "Another point that might be helpful right now is ...." (Refocus.)

No Comment:

Example: "Haven't you paid damage settlements in the past?"

Solution: "Each case is different and I don't think it would be productive to compare one with another. I'd be happy to discuss it in more detail when all the facts are in."

Off the Record:

Example: "Off the record, what's the real story?"

Solution: "There's only one issue for us right now and that's the victims' welfare." (Flagging.)

SOCKOs™ versus Qs & As

You may have noticed that in the preceding pages, I have referred to "examples" and "solutions" instead of "questions" and "answers." That's because there's a major difference in the way we use SOCKOs™ and the way some people use traditional "Question and Answer" briefings. As far as I'm concerned, there's no comparison. Here's a little exercise that will help convince you too.

Take the diagram in the book with the vertical line down the middle. Note the heading for the left-hand column — "Negative Questions." The heading for the right-hand column is "SOCKOs™!" — the exclamation mark is to remind you of the need for impact.

Focus first on the right-hand column.

This is the exact opposite of the Q and A system. I want you to focus on what you want to say, not the questions you may face.

QUESTIONS | SOCKOS™!

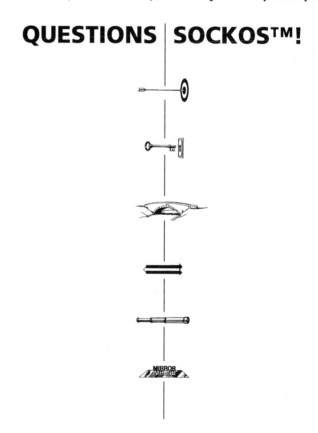

Figure 15: Questions SOCKOs™

So go ahead and list five, eight or ten SOCKOs™ that you want the world to know about. Next, in the left-hand column, write down the negative questions you think you might be asked by your critics and adversaries.

You may find that in some cases there's a direct correspondence between negative questions and SOCKOs™ you've prepared. If not, you are going to need a bridging or refocussing phrase to help you to deliver the information on the right-hand side of page.

In fact, you need to spend 90 percent of your time on the right-hand side of the page. That's because a journalist gets to ask the questions, edit the interview and write the story. And it's much the same in any other forum where you find yourself under pressure.

A judge can decide how much of your information is credible and deserves to be considered, and legislative committees and regulatory tribunals have similar powers. That means that your message has to be commensurately more powerful than the ability of reporters, judges, politicians and others to select from, and edit, what you say. The Q and A system can't help you here because it is focussed on the questions.

I've seen cabinet ministers on planes trying to wade through 50 or more pages of Qs & As in the hopes they'll be prepared for their next encounter with critics. But does anyone know whether the questions on Page 40 are really that much less important than those on Page 20? Who decides?

There are other drawbacks, too:

- If the minister doesn't hear a question phrased in the way it has been presented to her in her briefing, she may not know how to answer it and will miss an opportunity to advance her position or policies.

- Q & A briefing books rely on linear logic. Thus the cabinet minister will pay more attention to Pages 1–10 than Pages 40–50 because that's human nature.

Caring is vitally important.

- Aides and assistants don't like to present the boss with tough questions. Besides, there's always the danger of briefing documents becoming public and nobody wants to leave "negative" questions lying around in planes and taxis.

I like Henry Kissinger's approach to questions and answers. He once walked into a news conference and opened the proceedings by asking, "Does anyone have questions for my answers?" He recognized the importance of getting out his message — and so should you. Plug your SOCKO™ into the most appropriate question asked.

Caring, Knowledge and Action

These are your secret weapons when it comes to effective communication. Look on them as three separate pillars contributing to the power and effectiveness of your message.

There's no shortage of people who know what they're talking about and many of them can explain what they are doing, or will do in a particular situation. However, they forget about the caring, or empathetic, aspect of communication. As a result, they are not as effective as they could be.

Caring is vitally important.

Let's look at three well-known political leaders who came to prominence at about the same time in history and in similar cultures: Pierre Trudeau in Canada, Margaret Thatcher in Britain and Ronald Reagan in America.

Most people would agree that Pierre Trudeau was rated high on his knowledge, modest on action and low on caring. Margaret Thatcher was rated high on action, modest on knowledge and low on caring. Ronald Reagan was rated high on caring, modest on action and low on knowledge.

All three achieved considerable political and popular success, but only Ronald Reagan paid much attention to the caring aspect of communications and only he was known as "The Great Communicator."

This should be great news for all of us who worry about whether we have what it takes to succeed in public life or during a crisis. These three world leaders used vastly different techniques to arrive at the same successful place. You can too. Play the cards you have. Accentuate your strength, whether it is caring, knowledge or action. Accentuate what is most relevant and possible at the time. The moment you have an industrial accident, you won't have much knowledge and the only action you can take is to get the injured to hospital and stop a dangerous plant procedure. So you have to show caring. However, three days later, you need knowledge of the condition of the injured and three weeks later you need action on an inquiry and three months later you will probably need action to prevent further accidents.

EFFECTIVE COMMUNICATION

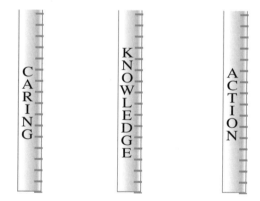

I CARE ABOUT ...

I KNOW ABOUT ...

I'M DOING ...

Figure 16: Effective Communication

I speculate that you can actually get more than full marks in these categories. If Reagan, Thatcher and Trudeau got high marks from the electorate in successive elections, yet were low on one or two of the categories, it must mean they got more than full marks in the one in which they excelled. Maybe Reagan got 115 percent for caring and Trudeau had 125 percent for knowledge and Thatcher received 130 percent for action. The extra marks compensated for a poor showing in other categories. So, play the cards you have and play them with vigour.

Here's an example of trying to succeed in each category: imagine hearing on television or radio that your local museum is to receive a gift of $20,000 from a generous benefactor, but there's no explanation of why the gift is being made or what the money will be used for. The main impact of such an announcement would be puzzlement. Caring and knowledge are completely absent and the action aspect is at the bare minimum. We can correct that by adding:

Caring: "We are giving $20,000 to the museum to help save some of its beautiful paintings."

Knowledge: "We are giving $20,000 to the museum to help save some of its beautiful paintings because their wooden frames are being eaten away by airborne pollutants."

Action: "We are giving $20,000 to the museum to help save some of its beautiful paintings because their wooden frames are being eaten away by airborne pollutants. Furthermore, we've sent samples of that wood for testing to see how best to protect it without harming the canvas."

Look how powerful that can be. The simple act of giving is transformed into something much more meaningful.

Words and Icons

People have very different ways in which they learn. The same technique does not work for everyone. You can probably recite your phone number quite quickly. But can you do it backwards? You probably can, but it will take you longer. That's because the mind absorbs certain information sequentially. Yet if I used the word "bicycle" you wouldn't first think of frame, handlebar, seat, wheel rims, spokes and hubs until all at once you had a complete image of a bicycle in your mind. Most objects you can visualize. Numbers we get sequentially.

There are even specific ways in which we get the sequence of numbers. Psychologists say that we can memorize up to seven things without great difficulty. That's one of the reasons phone numbers with area codes, or toll free numbers, are a little more difficult to remember. We sometimes couple numbers in sequence to make it easier to remember. My toll free number is 1-877-484-1667. I sometimes read the last four digits as "sixteen sixty-seven." But I would never say "one thousand, six hundred and sixty-seven." Surely, no one would recite my number as being "eighteen trillion, seven hundred and seventy-four million, eight hundred and forty-one thousand, six hundred and sixty-seven."

Very few people know what their address is backwards, or the sum of the digits in their phone number (mine is 5), and it doesn't matter. The point is, we absorb different information in different ways, even depending on the sort of people we are. Some prefer to learn visually, others orally, and so on.

So if the words and phrases I've used in the bridging techniques don't work for you, try using icons to achieve the same goal. You can use these as margin notes for a speech or presentation, or just as a doodle when you are being questioned to remind you how to frame your answer:

The bullseye directs you to the point you want to make or the topic you intend to stick to.

NOMENCLATURE

Figure 17: Nomenclature

The spectacles are used by musicians to remind them of a tricky bit of music. In other words, "Watch this ... things could go wrong here."

The telescope. You can look through either end of this to make things bigger or smaller. That's telescoping and microscoping. Examples are "All our customers are entitled to ..." and "One customer just the other day got a pleasant surprise when ...."

The easel and painting remind you to draw a word picture or tell a story to illustrate your point. Don't be afraid of using trigger phrases such as "Imagine this," "What we see is" or "Our vision is."

The hammer and anvil signify two things. By all means hammer away at the point you are trying to make. But if your are the one being hammered on, remove the anvil. It takes two sides to have a fight. Avoid a fight by bridging smoothly to one of your SOCKOs™.

The pyramid could just as easily be a cube, but I've already used a cube for a storyboard. A pyramid works because it's a geometric form with many faces, just as issues have many facets. But I urge you not to specify how many aspects before you start to enumerate or list them. It is all too easy to say something like the following: "There are three main reasons why this is important. Number One is ... blah, blah, blah. B is ... blah, blah, blah. And I forget Three." Once you launch into detailed lists you may find you have forgotten which number or letter comes next, or even whether it is a letter or number, and you may guess wrong. It is a risky technique. Just say there are many sides or facets and mention those that make your point.

The warped timepiece or clock serves as a reminder that while events and circumstances may be fixed in time, the ways they are viewed and judged can change with the passage of time. It can help you place things in context.

The scales represent balance. You may even want to use the introductory phrase, "On balance I think we can agree that ...."

The globe is there to remind you that you can use geography, just as you can use time, to provide context. An example might be, "Here's how we do it in Europe."

The wagon wheel consists of a hub from which spokes radiate out to a broader circumference. Or is it the other way around? You can choose the direction which best serves your purpose. Aren't there many issues that can be discussed from the inside out or from the outside in?

The two hands represent an old debating technique. If you set out two extreme views at opposite ends of the spectrum, then anything you articulate between those extreme positions will seem much more reasonable. An example might be, "Some people might think we should shut down the plant right now to immediately stop emissions. Others don't give emissions a second thought. We're in the middle because we want to keep creating jobs while lessening emissions."

The snowball or tumbleweed. It really doesn't matter which. It's there to remind you that if you feel you are "on a roll" and making progress with your audience — keep going!

Phrases or icons. It's up to you to choose which work better for you. The important thing is that you now have a workable system you can practise in preparation for the next time you come into contact with professional questioners, critics and adversaries. This is a system that can be used for dealing with regulatory bodies, the courts, investigating officers and media representatives.

As an example, let's focus on the media. Most people are wary of reporters and these days the media plays a very large role in deciding what is and isn't a crisis.

A television news story (and TV is where most of us get our news from) may appear to be short and simple, but it is not simple. The diagram of "A Reporter's Building Blocks" gives you an idea of how a fairly common TV story is constructed.

The newscaster introduces the item. The scene is set with voice-over narration of visuals (b-roll) leading to public reaction. This could be protesters, neighbours or people passing by. The third-party expert could be a professor, lawyer or other authority figure. The folk hero is someone who has become involved, either through personal experience or by witnessing the actual event. Sound clips, archival visuals and the reporter appearing on camera to make his or her summation fill out the rest of the item.

If you are the newsmaker, you can be squeezed between any two of these building blocks. And you won't have much time to make your point. It is a statistical fact that the average length of time devoted to your remarks in a television news item is just eight seconds. That isn't long, so you have to be good. However, if you are good you can have a huge influence on how the item finally emerges from the editing suite.

Reporters and editors are more likely to use clips of people who know what they're talking about and can explain issues briefly than those who don't and can't. They make choices and you can affect their choice.

A REPORTER'S BUILDING BLOCKS

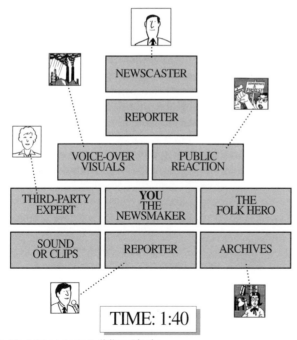

Figure 18: A Reporter's Building Blocks

A print news story has the shape of an inverted pyramid. It doesn't build from a broad base to a pointed conclusion, the way a police report sets out the facts and circumstances that led up to an incident. It is the exact opposite. It starts with the end result. "Hundreds of people are homeless today on the Yucatan Peninsula."

Later, you get the causes and additional details. There was a storm, boats were capsized and homes destroyed. It may have been the worst storm in history. Eyewitnesses said they were "shocked" at the devastation and emergency workers are on the scene.

At this rate you, the emergency worker, may not figure very prominently in the story in which you suddenly find yourself. The inverted pyramid story assumes that all the important components are close to the top and less important aspects are lower down. Editors working under deadline pressures can cut from the bottom of the story to fit a certain length without distorting the sense of the story.

Here again, your message and demeanour can decide whether you are depicted as peripheral or central to the story. The reporter could just as easily start his story, "Fast action by emergency crews is the best hope for hundreds of homeless people on the Yucatan Peninsula." The rest of the story is the same but the focus is now on a remedy, not the problem. If you're going to be up against SOCKOs™, especially with reporters, you need to have your own SOCKOs™!

THE ANATOMY OF
A NEWS STORY

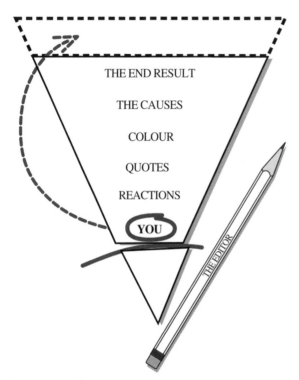

THE END RESULT

THE CAUSES

COLOUR

QUOTES

REACTIONS

YOU

THE EDITOR

Figure 19: Anatomy of a News Story

When Things Don't Work

We all have hopes, dreams and plans. They are personal, professional and for our families. We all spend a lot of time focussing on how to succeed. We read about the habits of successful people, watch biographies on TV and read the books that successful people write.

Perhaps there's some path we can follow that will ensure our success. We seem to be applying management and social science techniques to our daily lives. We measure ourselves. We want "quality" time with our partners and kids. We buy more labour-saving devices which often make us labour longer and harder. We take briefcases on vacation and to cottages.

But does life really boil down to a series of successes and failures to be tabulated daily? Is there anything terribly wrong with learning from failure? Can't progress be made regardless? We spend so much time planning our successes, but spend little time planning to learn from our failures.

This is dangerous territory for a trainer and CEO coach. I'm paid for quick fixes. My clients want the list of dos and don'ts, tips and tricks. They don't want to hear about exceptions. Luckily, I have a great list for my clients to follow. I believe that following my advice will lead to 80 to 90 percent success 95 percent of the time. Few CEOs want to pursue the next 5 or 10 or even 20 percent that is possible to bring full success.

So, I'd like to point to a framework that will require you to think about that marginal percentage for just a few minutes. Many people think that issues have a weight and temperature that can be measured and a solution of appropriate weight and temperature devised. Most of the time this is true. But I want to focus on the times that it isn't.

Take the issue of oil in water. Many issues, risk and public affairs managers have an instinct for how important an event spilling oil in water might be. They give it a mark out of 10 or assign a weight to it. If I said you were going to manage the 32nd largest oil spill in history, you might assign less weight to the event. If I said there would be so many oil spills in the world, your event was destined to decline to the 52nd largest over the following few years, you might be even less concerned. If there was a record fish catch in the area the year after your spill and another record the next year, you'd be even happier. And if I said scientists would try to find your spilled oil a couple of years later and had better luck finding old asphalt from 25 years before your spill, this comparison might make you think you could manage the event well.

Well, I'm describing the Exxon Valdez spill in Prince William Sound. Amazingly, this event is spoken of in the same breath as Chernobyl, Tylenol poisonings, Bhopal and other disasters where people died or where companies were the victims of terrorism. No one died in Valdez. A broken ankle was about the worst injury. Yet even some academics call it one of the worst environmental disasters in history. The PR company which now handles some of Exxon's work jokes that they can't do lectures anymore on how it was the worst-managed crisis in history.

So why is the Exxon Valdez oil spill in Prince William Sound in 1989 regarded as such a disaster when there is little, if any, scientific evidence to support such a view? The answer lies back at issue amplification and the diagram of the pinball machine in this book. It's also in research into risk done by the academic Roger Kasperson. Many observers view crises as things which happen on slow news days. This ignores all the other influential players in society.

Risk amplification theory has helped me develop my public policy pinball machine. In comes the issue of oil in water, just like the steel ball comes into a pinball machine. The perception of that event is influenced by media reports, lawyers seeking class action clients, environmentalists raising funds, aboriginals, fishery workers wanting compensation, legislators trying to get re-elected, regulators trying to show they're in control and many others. Just like the bumpers throw the steel ball around, these various actors throw around the issue of oil in water and it has different significance every time it hits a bumper.

One judge dealing with the Valdez case in his court is said to have referred to the oil spill as the "worst environmental disaster since Hiroshima." This is a preposterous statement, but judges are allowed to try to articulate the outrage of the community, if they wish, even if the statement has no basis in fact or science. Tens of thousands of people died instantly in Hiroshima and tens of thousands more died shortly thereafter. Someone will probably die this week in Hiroshima because of the atomic bomb dropped there during World War II. This comparison is silly, but it did influence people's risk perception.

And what does all this have to do with your management of such an event? Well, my friend and colleague, Ken Kansas, was Manager of Communication for Exxon during the spill and wrote words to the effect, "It's our oil, our ship, our fault, our captain. We'll pick it up and make it right." Few could ask for a more forthright and honest set of messages. Yet they didn't work. Why not? I surmise that the first four messages drew attention to the fact that this was a flagship company, known for technological excellence, an American-owned ship in U.S. waters with an American captain and crew. Normally these things happen under Panamanian flags, in rust buckets in the third world. The more these positive messages got out, the more there was shock and outrage.

The next two messages didn't help either. In the early weeks it became clear that they couldn't "pick it up and make it right." The ideal messages didn't work in a situation amplified by a dozen pressure groups.

Oil is made up of decomposed living matter. It biodegrades. Fish can swim under or around it, as can hairless mammals. Birds can fly over it. But fur-bearing mammals and birds that land in it usually die. There are some organisms on the ocean floor which seem to feed on oil and methane. Much scientific evidence, even at the time, suggested that leaving the oil alone would be the best course of action.

But I don't think any senior executive is prepared to have this discussion, live on CNN, at a Senate hearing or even in the Valdez town hall. Most CEOs would see the oil on the rocks and demand that the company be seen to be doing something, especially when reporters and politicians were demanding that something be done. Even if it harms the environment, everyone, including many environmentalists, are happier with action.

Have management and leadership really boiled down to the photo-
opportunity and sound bites on talk shows? Is this the best we can
do at the beginning of the 21st Century? I think it's important to focus
on what won't work, rather than trying to fit the same old solutions
into new problems.

Conclusion

I've had the privilege of coaching many well-known CEOs, ambassadors and politicians. They usually have little time to think beyond the immediate problem. We nail down a few hatches, bail out some water and sail on. Progress occurs, but at too slow a rate.

Francis Fukuyama, an economist at the Rand Corporation, wrote a book a while ago entitled *The End of History and the Last Man* in which he suggested that we are at the apex of human achievement. I wonder. As we find new ways to eliminate disease and suffering, we invent new forms of disease and suffering. The sale of illegal drugs in North America exceeds the output of some car manufacturers and the GDP of many countries. Thousands of children run away from home and are buried in unmarked graves because their parents don't know where they are or won't claim their bodies. Marriages fail, teachers don't teach, kids don't learn, and we sail on.

I wonder if this is good enough. I wonder if this is the best we can do.

Eric Kierans, a former politician and President of the Montréal Stock Exchange, has written a book entitled *Wrong End of the Rainbow: The Collapse of Free Enterprise in Canada* in which he suggests that the modern corporation is so large and complex that it is beyond the control of its CEO and Board of Directors. Certainly we have known for some time that political leaders have few levers they can pull to influence their own jurisdictions. I wonder if some of our current management techniques are smokescreens designed to mask the impotence of the modern leader. Perhaps if you can't really do anything, at least you can buy the latest management best-seller and whip your organization into a frenzy over some trend that will be gone in a year. The "Hawthorne effect" states that a change in environment will yield an increase in productivity, so why not?

I often turn to W. B. Yeats' poetry to understand leaders. His lines from "The Second Coming" surface when I consider these topics:

"The best lack all conviction, while the worst are full of passionate intensity."

It often seems that the best we can do is be passionately intense about things no one can change.

Americans worry about one of the world's last command economies 90 miles from its border. Yet there are many dozens of corporations with GDPs larger than Cuba's. Does anyone worry about that?

There is a real personal danger to me in raising these issues. I'm a trainer and coach. I am supposed to have answers. In fact, I have so many answers I sometimes don't hear the questions they're supposed to fit. Clients like it when I have the "right" course of action after only half an hour on the job. That's proper crisis management. I don't think they like it when I have more questions than they do. But there is greater danger than my asking questions that I might not have answers for. This greater danger is allowing CEOs, cabinet ministers and heads of government to get away with thinking they've addressed a problem when what they've really done is just made it through the day. It's too easy to satisfy the average journalist, legislative committee or regulator and move on. Is this the best we can do?

The real danger in my line of work is that the answers and solutions I sell actually work, and many work even in the long term. Because everyone is busy, the quick fix is at a premium. The e-mail, courier, voice mail, Blackberry and cell phone system does not allow for thought and reflection. Are we really all too busy for professional development, or even to do a thorough job?

The SOCKO™ system is designed to save time and allow for some thought. Instead of 50 pages of Qs & As, perhaps two pages of SOCKOs™ might allow the cabinet minister or CEO to think about the issue instead of just talk about it. Perhaps pre-written SOCKOs™ would allow the company in crisis to focus on doing the right thing instead of just saying the right thing. Perhaps we can focus more on what we need to do, rather than promoting the only thing we seem able to do.

These are some of my hopes and what is motivating me in the last half of my training and coaching career. I hope they motivate you.

Bibliography

Abe, Kitao (undated) "Levels of Trust and Reactions to Various Sources of Information in Catastrophic Situations", *Disasters:Theory and Research*,Tokyo University of Foreign Studies,Japan, pp.147-158.

Adams, W.C. (1986) "Whose lives count?:TV coverage of natural disasters.", *Journal of Communication*, Spring 36(2): 113-122, in Sood, R., Stockdale, G. and Rogers, E.M., (1987) "How the News Media Operate in Natural Disasters", *Journal of Communication*, 37(3) pp. 27-41.

American Psychiatric Association (1980, 1987, 1994) *Diagnostic and Statistical Manual of Mental Disorders*, 3rd edn, 3rd edn revised & 4th edn,Washington, DC:APA.

Anderson, Karen, Manuel, Gardenio (1994) "Gender Differences in Reported Stress Response to the Loma Prieta Earthquake", *Sex Roles,* Vol. 30, Nos. 9/10, 1994, Plenum Publishing Corporation.

Aptekar, Lewis (1990) "A Comparison of the Bicostal Disasters of 1989", *Behavior Science Research*, HRAF, pp. 73-101.

Beck, Ulrich (1992) "From Industrial Society to the Risk Society: Questions of Survival, Social Structure and Ecological Enlightenment", from *Theory, Culture & Society*, vol. 9 London: Sage Publications, pp. 97-123.

Benveniste, G. (1977, 1983) "Bureaucracy", San Francisco: Boyd & Fraser in Comfort, L.K., "Turning Conflict into Cooperation: Organizational Designs for Community Response in Disasters", *Int. J. Ment. Health*,Vol. 19, No. 1, pp. 89-108 M.E. Sharpe, Inc.

Berg, David H. (1987) "Preparing Witnesses", *Litigation, Winter*, Volume 13, Number 2, pp. 13-16.

Berke, Philip R., Beatley, Timothy (1992) "Planning for Earthquakes, Risk, Politics and Policy",The Johns Hopkins University Press, Baltimore and London.

Blaufarb, Herbert, Levine, Jules (1972) "Crisis Intervention in an Earthquake", *Social Work*, July, 16(4).

Blomkvist, Anna-Cristina, Sjöberg, Lennart (Date Unavailable) "Risk and accident reports in the mass media", *Mass Media Reports*.

Bohère, G. (1984) "Profession: Journalist, A Study on the Working Conditions of Journalists", *International Labour Office*, Geneva.

Bolton, Patricia A. & Olson, Jon L. (1990) "Organizational Theory And Emergency Management: Can Risks From Industrial Hazards Be Contained?", *International Sociological Association (ISA)*.

Bonner, W. Allan (1999) "Given Its Size and Impact, Why is the *Exxon Valdez* Oil Spill so Prominent in Disaster Literature?" Leicester University, Leicester England: MSc Dissertation for the Scarman Centre for the Study of Public Order.

Bonner, W. Allan (1983) "The Rise and Decline of Public Broadcasting and the Dream of Regional Representation, 1900 - 1982: A Public Policy Question." York University, Toronto Ontario: Master of Arts research paper.

Bonner, W. Allan (1997) "How Psychological, Sociological and Cultural Theories of Risk Differ", The Centre for Training in Risk and Crisis Management, Toronto, 2001.

Bonner, W. Allan (1997) "Does the Management of Crisis Suggest a Failure of Security?", The Centre for Training in Risk and Crisis Management, Toronto, 2001.

Bonner, W. Allan (1997) "What influence might cultural, spatial and temporal distance exert on our capacity to learn from past disasters?", The Centre for Training in Risk and Crisis Management, Toronto, 2001.

Bonner, W. Allan (1998) "Public Participation is a Prerequisite of Effective Disaster Management", The Centre for Training in Risk and Crisis Management, Toronto, 2001.

Bonner, W. Allan (1989) "Political Conventions and the Media," in Two Countries, Two Conventions, Two Delegates, A Guidebook, Marion C. Salinger, Editor., Duke University Center for International Studies.

Boutacoff, D. (1989) "Real world lessons in seismic safety", *EPRI Journal*, June, p. 23.

Bradshaw, John (1992) "Homecoming, Reclaiming and Championing your Inner Child, Bantam Books, N.Y.

Brearley, Nigel (1992) "Public Order, Safety & Crowd Control", *Intersec*, Vol 2, Issue 1, May, 4-6.

British Psychological Society (1990), "Psychological Aspects of Disaster", *British Psychological Society*, Leicester, St. Andrews House, September.

Bromet, E., Parkinson, D., Schulberg, H.C., Dunn, L. (1980) "Three Mile Island: Mental Health Findings." Pittsburgh, PA: *Western Psychiatric Institute and Clinic and the University of Pittsburgh*.

Brown, Michael (1979) "Laying Waste: The Poisoning of America by Toxic Chemicals", New ork: *Pantheon Books* in Mazur, Allan, (1984) "The Journalists and Technology: Reporting about Love Canal and Three Mile Island", *The Journalist and Technology*, Minerva, 22:45-66.

Browning, Larry D. and Shetler, Judy C. (1982) "Communication in Crisis, Communication in Recovery: A Postmodern Commentary On The *Exxon Valdez* Disaster", *International Journal of Mass Emergencies and Disasters*, (November), 10(3): 477-98.

Burke, Edmund (1968) "Citizen Participation Strategies", *Journal of the American Institute of Planners*, 34, 287-294 in "Six Propositions on Public Participation and Their Relevance for Risk Communications", Kasperson, Roger E., (1986), *Journal of the Society for Risk Analysis*, Volume 6, Number 3, pp. 275-281.

Busch, Lisa (1991) "Science Under Wraps in Prince William Sound" *Science* Vol.252

Bytwerk, R.L. (1979) "The SST controversy: A case study of the rhetoric of technology" *Central States Speech Journal*, 30, in "Scientific argument in organizational crisis communication: the case of Exxon (Exxon Corp.), Sellnow, Timothy L. (1993), *Argumentation and Advocacy*, Summer 1993 30(1):28(15).

Christopher, P. (1997) "Was the E. Coli Outbreak Predictable?", *Journal of the Royal Society of Health* 117(1):40.

Clarke, Lee (1993) "The Disqualification Heuristic: When Do Organizations Misperceive Risk?" *Research in Social Problems and Public Policy*, Volume 5, JAI Press Inc.

CNN (1989) "The Big Spill", 15 April.

Cocking, Clive (1980) *Following the Leaders*, Toronto: Doubleday Canada Limited.

Cohen, Maurie J. (1995) "Technological disasters and natural resource damage assessment: an evaluation of the *Exxon Valdez* oil spill", (1989 Alaskan disaster), *Land Economics*, February, 71(1): 65(18).

Cohen, Maurie J. (1993) "Economic Impact of an Environmental Accident: A Time-Series Analysis of the *Exxon Valdez* Oil Spill in South-Central Alaska", *Sociological-Spectrum*, 13(1): 35-63.

Collier, T.K. et al. In *Exxon Valdez Oil Spill Symposium*; Feb 2-5, 1993, Anchorage, AK; Abstracts, pp. 235-38 in Wolfe, Douglas A., et. al. (1994) "The Fate of the Oil Spilled from the *Exxon Valdez*", Environment, Science, Technology, Vol. 28(13).

Combs, Barbara and Slovic, Paul (undated) "Newspaper Coverage of Causes of Death", *Journalism Quarterly*, p. 837- 849.

Comfort, Louise K. (1990) "Turning Conflict into Cooperation: Organizational Designs for Community Response in Disasters", *Int. J. Ment. Health*, Vol. 19, No. 1, pp. 89-108 M.E. Sharpe, Inc.

Covello, V.T., Menkes, J. and Nehnevajsa, J. (1982) "Risk Analysis, Philosophy, and the Social and Behavioral Sciences: Reflections on the Scope of Risk Analysis Research", *Journal of the Society for Risk Analysis*, Volume 2, Number 2, pp. 53-57.

Covello, V.T., Sandman, P.M., and Slovic, P. (1988) "Risk Communication, Risk Statistics, and Risk Comparisons: A Manual for Plant Managers", Washington, D.C.: Chemical Manufacturers Association, in Roth, Emilie, (1990) "What Do We Know About Making Risk Comparisons?", *Journal of the Society for Risk Analysis*, Volume 10, Number 3, pp. 375-387.

Crable R.E. & Vibbert S.L. (1985) "Managing issues and influencing public policy" Public Relations Review, 11, 3-15, in "Scientific argument in organizational crisis communication: the case of Exxon (Exxon Corp.), in Sellnow, Timothy L. (1993), *Argumentation and Advocacy*, Summer 1993 30(1):28(15).

Crouse, Timothy (1978) "The Boys on the Bus, New York", Ballantine Books.

Crow, Patrick (1989) "*Exxon Valdez* spill spawns a batch of legislation governing tankers," *Oil and Gas Journal*, July 31.

Cumming, R.B. (1981) "Is Risk Assessment A Science?" *Journal of the Society for Risk Analysis*, Volume 1, Number 1, pp. 1-3.

Dahlin, Jeffrey A. (1989) "Oil Shock", *Business and Economic Review*, 35(4): 3-7.

Daley, Patrick & O'Neill, Dan (1991) "'Sad is too mild a word': Press Coverage of the *Exxon Valdez* Oil Spill", *Journal of Communication* 41(4), Autumn.

Davidson, Art (1990) "In the Wake of the *Exxon Valdez*", Sierra Club Books, San Francisco

de Man, A., & Simpson-Housley, P. (1987) "Factors in perception of earthquake hazard", *Perceptual and Motor Skills*, 815-820, in Dooley, David, Catalano, Ralph, Mishra, Shiraz, Serxner, Seth (1992) "Earthquake Preparedness: Predictors in a Community Survey", *Journal of Applied Social Psychology*, V.H. Winston & Son, Inc.

Demers, David Pearce, Nichols, Suzanne (1987) "Precision Journalism: A Practical Guide", Beverly Hills, California: *Sage Publications Inc.*

Derby, Stephen L. and Keeney, Ralph L. (1981) "Risk Analysis: Understanding 'How Safe is Safe Enough'?", *Risk Analysis*, Vol. 1, No. 3.

Dev, Krishan (1994) The 5th Column, "Tanking Up", *Far Eastern Economic Review*, April 28.

Diringer, Elliot (1990) "The Troubled Coast Guard: Critics Say It Shares Responsibility for the Valdez Oil Spill", *San Francisco Chronicle*, final ed., March 23, p.A1. NEXIS in Smith, Conrad (1993), "News Sources and Power Elites in News Coverage of the *Exxon Valdez*", *Journalism Quarterly*, Summer, 70(2), pp.393-403.

Dombrowsky, Wolf R. (1995) "Again and Again: Is a Disaster What We Call 'Disaster'? Some Conceptual Notes on Conceptualizing the Object of Disaster Sociology", *International Journal of Mass Emergencies and Disasters*, 13(3):241-54.

Dooley, David, Catalano, Ralph, Mishra, Shiraz, Serxner, Seth (1992)"Earthquake Preparedness: Predictors in a Community Survey", *Journal of Applied Social Psychology*, V.H. Winston & Son, Inc., pp. 451-470.

Douglas, Mary and Wildavsky, Aaron (1982) "How Can We Know the Risks We Face? Why Risk Selection Is a Social Process", *Journal of the Society for Risk Analysis*, Volume 2, Number 2, pp. 49-51.

Dyer, Samuel Coad, Jr., Miller, M. Mark, Bonne, Jeff (1991) "Wire service coverage of the *Exxon Valdez* crisis", *Public Relations Review*, (Spring) 17(1): 27(10).

Economist, The (1995) "The flowers of Kobe", January 21st, 35:2.

Erikson, Kai, T. (1978) "Everything in its Path", Simon & Shuster.

Esters, Stephanie D. (1997) "Coverage need seen for smaller-scale leaks, spills", *National Underwriter Property and Casualty/Risk and Benefits Management*, 101(3): 3,16.

Estes, James A. (1991) "Catastrophes and Conservation: Lessons from Sea Otters and the *Exxon Valdez*," *Science*, Vol. 254.

Etkin, Dagmar Schmidt (1997) "Oil Spill Intelligence Report" International Oil Spill Statistics: 1996, *Cutter Information Corp.*

Everest, Larry (1986) "Behind the Poison Cloud. Union Carbide's Bhopal Massacre", Chicago, ILL: *Banner Press*.

***Exxon Valdez* Oil Spill Trustee Council** (EVOSTC) (1992) "Summary of Injury", *Alaska's Marine Resources*, 7(3): 2-11.

Fennell, D. (1988) "Investigation into the King's Cross Underground Fire", *Her Majesty's Stationary Office*, (Dept. of Transport). London.

Fessenden-Raden, June, Fitchen, Janet M., and Heath, Jenifer S.
(1987) "Providing Risk Information in Communities: Factors
Influencing What Is Heard and Accepted", *Science, Technology
& Human Values*, Summer/Fall, pp.94- 101.

Feyerabend, P. (1975) "Against Method: Outline of an Anarchistic
Theory of Knowledge", *New York Free Press*.

Fink, Steven (1986) "Crisis Management", Amacom (U.S) & Toronto:
Prentice Hall.

Fischhoff, Baruch (1985) "Managing Risk Perception" *Issues in
Science and Technology*, Fall, pp. 84-96.

Fischhoff, Baruch (1987) "Treating the Public with Risk Communications:
A Public Health Perspective", *Science, Technology, & Human
Values*, Volume 12, Issues 3 & 4 (Summer/Fall).

Ford, D.F. (1986) "Meltdown: The Secret Papers on the Atomic Energy
Commission", *New York: Simon and Schuster* in Clarke, Lee (1993)
"The Disqualification Heuristic: When Do Organizations Misperceive
Risk?" *Research in Social Problems and Public Policy*, Volume 5,
JAI Press Inc.

Frosdick, Steve (1995) "Safety Cultures in British Stadia and Sporting
Venues", *Disaster Prevention and Management*, Volume 4 -
Number 4, pp.13-21, MCB University Press.

Galen, Michele & Cahan, Vicky (1989) "Getting Ready for Exxon vs.
Practically Everybody", *Business Week*, (Industrial/Technology
Edition) Number 3125: 190-194.

Gans, Herbert J. (1979) "Deciding What's News", New York: *Pantheon*.

Gephart, Jr., Robert P. (1984) "Making sense of Organizationally
Based Environmental Disasters", *Journal of Management*, 10(2)
pp. 205-225.

Gibney, Frank and Pope, Richard (1979) "Catastrophe! When Man Loses Control", New York: *Bantam/Britannica Books* in Mazur, Allan, (1984) "The Journalists and Technology: Reporting about Love Canal and Three Mile Island", *The Journalist and Technology,* Minerva, 22:45-66.

Giel, R. (1990) "The Psychosocial Aftermath of Two Major Disasters in the Soviet Union", *Journal of Traumatic Stress,* Vol. 4, No. 3, 1991.

Gilmore, Frank (1988) "Dealing with the press in a serious emergency", *Supervision,* April.

Gipson, William E. (1989) "Pogo's Gipson: an oilman views the *Exxon Valdez* tanker spill", **Oil and Gas Journal,** 15 May.

Gottschalk, Jack A. (1993) "Crisis Response Inside Stories on Managing Image Under Siege", Detroit: Visible Ink Press.

Griffiths, Richard F. (ed) (1981) "Dealing with Risk: The Planning Management and Acceptability of Technological Risk", "Introduction: The nature of risk assessment", New York: *Wiley,* pp.1-19.

Grover, Ronald (1989) "Fighting Back: The Resurgence of Social Activism", *Business Week,* (Industrial/Technology Edition) Number 3106: 34-35.

Habermas, Jürgen (1989) "The Structural Transformation of the Public Sphere: An Inquiry into a Category of Bourgeois Society", Cambridge, Mass.: MIT Press.

Halberstam, David (1979) "The Powers That Be", New York: *Alfred A. Knopf, Inc.*

Hamlin, Sonya (1985) "Preparing a Witness to Testify", *ABA Journal. The Lawyer's Magazine,* April, Volume 71, pp. 81-84.

Hannaford, Peter (1986) "Talking Back to the Media", *Facts on File Publications*, New York.

Hart, Roderick P. (1994) "Seducing America: How Television Charms the Modern Voter", New York: *Oxford University Press*.

Heising, C.D., and George, V.P. (1986) "Nuclear Financial Risk: Economy Wide Cost of Reactor Accidents", *Energy Policy*, 14, p.45-52.

Hill, Stephen and Bryan, Jane (1997) "The Economic Impact of the Sea Empress Spillage", *Welsh Economy Research Unit*, Cardiff Business School, 227-233.

Holloway, Marguerite (1993) "Sound Science? Researchers still sparring over effects of *Exxon Valdez*", *Scientific American, August*, 269:20, New York.

Home Office, The (1994) "Easingwold Papers No.8, A Digest of Well-Known Disasters", *Home Office Emergency Planning College*, York, UK.

HSE (1989) Risk Criteria for Land Use Planning in the Vicinity of Major Industrial Hazards", *London: HMSO*, pp.1-21.

Husband, S. (1993) "Disaster Survivors Talking", *Options*, August: 44-47.

Irvine, Robert B. (1987) "When You are the Headline", Dow Jones Irwin (U.S.) & Toronto: *Oxford University Press*.

Irving, John A. (ed) (1962) "Mass Media in Canada", Toronto: *The Ryerson Press*.

Iyengar, Shanto and Kinder, Donald R. (1987) "News That Matters", Chicago: *The University of Chicago Press*.

James, W.I. (1955) "Pragmatism", New York: *Meridian Books*.

Johnson, Daniel (1993) "Crisis management: forewarned is fore-armed", *Journal of Business Strategy*, March-April, 14(2): 58(6).

Jorgensen, Joseph G., McCleary, Richard and McNabb, Steven (1985) "Social Indicators in Native Village Alaska", *Human Organization*, 44:2-17.

Kasperson, Roger E. et al. (1988) "The Social Amplification of Risk: A Conceptual Framework", *Society for Risk Analysis*, 8 January, 8(2): 177-187.

Kasperson, Roger E.(1986) "Six Propositions on Public Participation and Their Relevance for Risk Communications", *Journal of the Society for Risk Analysis*, Volume 6, Number 3, pp. 275-281.

Keeble, John (1991) "Out of the Channel: The *Exxon Valdez* Oil Spill in Prince William Sound" (New York: Harper Collins).

Knight, Rory F. & Pretty, Deborah J. (undated) "The Impact of Catastrophes on Shareholder Value", *Sedgwick Group*, University of Oxford, London.

Kovoor-Misra, Sarah (1995) "A Multidimensional Approach to Crisis Preparation for Technical Organizations: Some Critical Factors", *Technological Forecasting and Social Change*, 48(2): 143-160.

Kvenvolden, Keith A., Carlson, Paul R., Threlkeld, Charles N., Warden, Augusta (1993) "Possible connection between two Alaskan catastrophes occurring 25 yrs apart (1964 and 1989)", *Geology*, (September) v. 23, pp. 813-816.

Kvenvolden, K.A.; Hostettler, F.D., Rapp, J.B.; and Carlson, P.R. (1993) "Hydrocarbons in oil residues on beaches of islands of Prince William Sound, Alaska, *Marine Pollution Bulletin*, v.16, pp. 24-29.

Lambourne, Robert (1997) "Public Warning System and The Chemical Industry", *From International Disaster and Emergency Response: IDER '97 Conference Proceedings.*

Langer, John (1998) "Tabloid Television. Popular Journalism and the 'Other News'", *New York Routledge.*

Lash, Scott, Szerszynski, Bronislaw and Wynne, Brian (1996) "Risk, Environment & Modernity: Towards a New Ecology", London: *Sage Publications, Inc.*

Levine, Allan (1993) "Scrum Wars: The Prime Ministers and the Media", Toronto: *Dundurn Press.*

Lifton, R.J. (1983) "Responses of Survivors to Man-made Catastrophes", *Bereavement Care* 2:2-6.

Lindblom, C.E. (1977) "Politics and markets", New York: Basic Books quoted in Comfort, L.K., "Turning Conflict Into Cooperation".

Little, Ronald L. and Robbins, Lynn A. (1984) "Effects Of Renewable Resource Harvest Disruptions on Socioeconomic and Sociocultural Systems: St Laurence Island. Anchorage; Alaska Outer Continental Shelf Region", *Mineral Management Service.*

Logue, J.N., Melik, M.E., and Hansen, H. (1981) "Research Issues and Directions in the Epidemiology of Health Effects of Disasters", *Epidemiologic Reviews* 3:140-162.

Luton, Harry (1985) "Effects of Renewable Resource Harvest Disruptions on Socioeconomic and Sociocultural Systems: Chukchi Sea, Anchorage: Alaska Outer Continental Shelf Region", *Minerals Management Service.*

MacQueen, Ken (1999) "The real victims of the *Exxon Valdez*", *National Post*, March 6, B4-5.

Marshall, Eliot (1989) News and Comment, "Valdez: The Predicted Oil Spill," *Science*, vol.244, April 7.

Mazur, Allan (1984) "The Journalists and Technology: Reporting about Love Canal and Three Mile Island", *The Journalist and Technology*, Minerva, 22:45-66.

McConnell, Malcolm (1987) "Challenger. A Major Malfunction", Garden City, New York: *Doubleday & Company, Inc.*

McDermott, J. (1974) "Technology: Opiate of the Intellectuals", in E. Mendelsohn (ed.), *Technology and Man's Future*. pp. 107-33.

McElhaney, James W. (1992) "Preparing Witnesses for Depositions", *ABA Journal*, June, pp.85-86.

McLaughlin, Paul (1986) "Asking Questions. The art of the media interview", Vancouver, B.C.: *International Self- Counsel Press Ltd.*

McLoy, John J. (1976) "The Great Oil Spill", New York: *Chelsea House Publishers.*

McLuhan, Marshall (1964) "Understanding Media", Mentor, New York.

Mendelsohn, E. (ed.) (1974) "Technology and Man's Future", New York: St. Martin's Press.

Mooney, Michael M. (1972) "The Hindenburg", New York: *Bantam Books.*

Moore, Tony (1992) "Crowd Management: Learning From History", *The Police Journal*, April. pp. 99-108

Morgan, M. Granger, Slovic, Paul, Nair, Indira, Geisler, Dan, MacGregor, Donald, Fischhoff, Baruch, Lincoln, David, Florig, Keith (1985) "Powerline Frequency Electric and Magnetic Fields: Pilot Study of Risk Perception", *Journal of the Society for Risk Analysis*, Volume 5, Number 2, pp. 139-149.

Munk, Nina (1994) "We're partying hearty!" *Forbes,* October 24,
154(10): 84-90.

Nelkin, Dorothy (1985) "The Language of Risk: Conflicting
Perspectives on Occupational Health", Nelkin, Dorothy, Editor.,
Beverly Hills, California, *Sage Publications, Inc.*

Neustatter, A. (1996) "When jury service can become a trial", You: The
Mail on Sunday, 28 July: pp. 34-7.

Nulty, Peter (1989) "The Future of Big Oil", *Fortune*, 8 May, 119(10):
46-49.

O'Clair, C.E. et al. *"Exxon Valdez* Oil Spill Symposium", Feb. 2-5 1993,
Anchorage, AK; Abstracts, pp. 55-56, Wolfe, Douglas A., et. al. (1994)
"The Fate of the Oil Spilled from the *Exxon Valdez*", *Environment,
Science,* Technology, Vol. 28(13)

O'Connell, Jeffrey and Meyers, Arthur (1966) "Safety Last", New
York: *Avon Books.*

OECD Nuclear Agency (1987) "Chernobyl and the Safety of Nuclear
Reactors in OECD Countries", *Organization for Economic
Cooperation and Development,* Paris.

Oil and Gas Journal (1993) "Contest brewing over Exxon fines",
August 91(35): 19.

Pain, Stephanie (1993) "The two faces of the Exxon disaster" *New
Scientist*, May 22.

**Palinkas, Lawrence A., Downs, Michael A., Petterson, John S. and
Russell, John** (1993) "Social, Cultural, and Psychological Impacts
of the *Exxon Valdez* Oil Spill", *Human Organization, Society for
Applied Anthropology*, Spring 52(1).

Parkinson, F. (1993) "Post-Trauma Stress", London: *Sheldon Press/SPCK.*

Pauchant, Thierry C., Mitroff, Ian I. (1992) "Transforming the Crisis-Prone Organization", *Jossey-Bass Inc.*, San Francisco, CA.

Pavlik, John V. (1987) "Public Relations. What Research Tells Us", Newbury Park, California: *SAGE Publications, Inc.*

Peaks, Martha H. (1990) [Editor of] "The Alaskan Oil Spill: Lessons in Crisis Management", *Management Review*, April.

Perrow, C. (1984) "Normal Accidents: Living With High Risk Technologies", New York: *Basic Books* in Clarke, Lee (1993) "The Disqualification Heuristic: When Do Organizations Misperceive Risk?" *Research in Social Problems and Public Policy*, Volume 5, JAI Press Inc.

Phillips, Brenda D., PhD (1992) "Planning for the Expected: Evacuation in a Chemical Emergency", *Disaster Management*, 4:2.

Pidgeon, N. (1991) "Safety Culture and Risk Management in Organizations", *Journal of Cross Cultural Psychology*, 22(1) pp. 129-140.

Pidgeon, N.F. (1992) "The Psychology of Risk", in D.I. Blockley (Ed). *Engineering Safety*. Maidenhead: McGraw-Hill. pp167-185.

Plummer, K. (1990) "Documents of Life: An Introduction to the Problems and Literature of a Humanistic Method", London: *Unwin Hyman.*

Porfiriev, Boris (1996) "Social Aftermath and Organizational Response to a Major Disaster: The Case of the 1995 Sakhalin Earthquake in Russia", *Journal of Contingencies and Crisis Management*, Blackwell Publishers Ltd., December 4(4), pp. 218-27.

Porter, G. and Brown, J. (1991) "Global Environmental Politics", Boulder CO: *Westview.*

Quarantelli, Henry in Roush, Wade (1993) "Learning from Technology" *Technology Review*, MIT, Cambridge, MA, August/September.

Real, Terrence (1997) "I Don't Want to Talk About It", Fireside, New York.

Richardson, Bill "Socio-technical Disasters: Profile and Prevalence", *Sheffield Business School*, Sheffield, UK.

Ries, Al, Trout, Jack (1981) "Positioning: The Battle for Your Mind", *McGraw-Hill Book Company*.

Roberts, Karlene H., Libuser, Carolyn (1993) "From Bhopal to Banking: Organizational Design Can Mitigate Risk", *Organizational-dynamics*, Spring, 21(4): 15-26.

Roberts, Leslie (1989) News and Comment, "Long, Slow Recovery Predicted for Alaska" *Science*, vol.244, April 7.

Rogers, Alison (1994) "Where The Valdez Players Are Now, Five Years Later", *Fortune*, April 4.

Rohmer, Richard (1984) "Massacre 747: The Story of Korean Air Lines Flight 007, *Paperjacks*, Markham, Ontario, May.

Rosenthal, Uriel, et al. (1994) "Complexity in Urban Crisis Management: Amsterdam's Response to the Bihlmer Air Disaster", *James & James*, London.

Roth, Emilie (1990) "What Do We Know About Making Risk Comparisons?", *Journal of the Society for Risk Analysis*, Volume 10, Number 3, pp. 375-387.

Roush, Wade (1993) "Learning from Technology" *Technology Review*, MIT, Cambridge, MA, August/September.

Royal Society (1992) "Risk: Analysis, Perception and Management", Royal Society Study Group, 135-92, The Royal Society, London.

Ruckelshaus, W.D. (1984) "Risk in a Free Society", *Journal of the Society for Risk Analysis,* Volume 4, Number 3, pp. 157-162.

Russell, M. and Gruber, M. (1987) "Risk Assessment in Environmental Policy-Making", *Science,* Volume 236, April, pp. 286-290.

Rutherford, Paul (1978) "The Making of the Canadian Media", Toronto: *McGraw-Hill Ryerson.*

Sandman, Peter M., Sachman (1985) "Getting to Maybe: Some Communications Aspects of Siting Hazardous Waste Facilities", *Seton Hall Legislative Journal,* Vol.9:437, 1985].

Sauerhaft, Stan, Atkins, Chris (1989) "Image Wars, Protecting Your Company When There's No Place to Hide", *John Wiley & Sons.*

Savage, J.A. (1989) "IS bridge over oily waters", *Computer World, Manager's Journal,* May 29.

Schlossberg, Howard (1991) "Americans passionate about the environment? Critic says that's 'nonsense'." *Marketing News,* 16 September, 25(19):8(1).

Schmertz, Herb (1986) "Good-bye to the Low Profile, The Art of Creative Confrontation", *Little, Brown,* Boston.

Schnoor, Jerald (1991) "The Alaska oil spill: Its effects and lessons", *Environment, Science and Technology,* 1990 American Chemical Society. 25(1):14(1).

Scott, J. (1990) "A Matter of Record", Cambridge: *Polity Press.*

Seeger, M.W. (1987) "The Challenger tragedy and search for legitimacy", *Central States Journal* (37: 147-157).

Seibert, Fred S., Peterson, Theodore; Schramm, Wilbur, (1974) "Four Theories of the Press", Urbana: University of Illinois Press.

Selkirk, Alexander M., Jr. (1992) "Witness Preparation: Key to a Successful Trial Strategy", *New York State Bar Journal*, February, pp. 18-23.

Sellnow, Timothy L. (1993) "Scientific argument in organizational crisis communication: the case of Exxon (Exxon Corp.), *Argumentation and Advocacy*, Summer 1993 30(1):28(15).

Shao, Maria (1990) "Everybody cleaned up. That's the problem", *Business Week* (August).

Sharlin, Harold Issadore (1986) "EDB: A Case Study in the Communication of Health Risk, *Risk Analysis*, 6, 61-68.

Shore, James H., Tatum, Ellie L., and Wollmer, William M. (1986) "Evaluation of Mental Effects of Disaster", Mount St. Helen's Eruption, *American Journal of Public Health* 76: 76-83.

Shore, James H. (1986) "The Mount St. Helen's Stress Response Syndrome" in *Disaster Stress Studies: New Methods and Findings*, James H. Shore, ed. 77-98, Washington, D.C.: American Psychiatric Press.

Singer, E. and Endreny, P. (1987) "Reporting Hazards: Their Benefits and Costs", *Journal of Communication*, 37(3) pp. 10-25.

Sipes, Joel D. (1990) "The Alaskan Oil Spill: Lessons in Crisis Management", *Management Review*, April.

Small, William J. (1991) "*Exxon Valdez*: how to spend billions and still get a black eye", *Public Relations Review* (Spring) 17(1): 9 (17).

Smith, Anthony (1980) "Newspapers and Democracy", *The Massachusetts Institute of Technology*.

Smith, Conrad (1993) "News Sources and Power Elites in News Coverage of the *Exxon Valdez*", *Journalism Quarterly*, Summer, 70(2), pp. 393-403.

Smith, Elizabeth (1986) "Psychosocial Consequences of a Disaster" in *Disaster Stress Studies: New Methods and Findings,* James Shore Ed., Washington, D.C.: *American Psychiatric Press,* pp. 51-76.

Sood, Rahul, Stockdale, Geoffrey and Rogers, Everett M. (1987) "How the News Media Operate in Natural Disasters", *Journal of Communication,* 37(3), Summer, pp. 27-41.

Sorensen, et. al. (1987) "Impacts of Hazardous Technology: The Psycho-Social Effects of Restarting", TMI State University of New York Press, Albany.

Stanton, Alex (1989) "Management can keep a crisis from turning into a calamity," *Oil & Gas Journal,* 8 May, pp. 15-16.

Stone, Richard (1993) "Dispute Over *Exxon Valdez* Cleanup Data Gets Messy", *Science,* (May) Vol. 260.

Stevens, William (1990) "The Alaskan Oil Spill: Lessons in Crisis Management", *Management Review,* April.

Swire, Jane (1995) "The aftermath of disaster", *British Medical Journal,* 23-30 December, 311:1688-9.

Taaffe, Gerald (1966) "The Great Beer Scare", *McLeans,* (month unavailable).

Tataryn, Lloyd (1985) "The Pundits; Power, Politics and the Press", *Deneau Publishers,* Toronto.

Thomas, Bob (1971) "Winchell", Garden City, New York: *Doubleday & Company, Inc.*

Toft, B. and Reynolds, S. (1994) "Learning From Disasters: A Management Approach", Oxford: *Butterworth Heinemann.*

Troy, Gil (1991) "See How They Ran: The Changing Role of the Presidential Candidate", New York: *The Free Press.*

Trueman, Peter (1980) "Smoke & Mirrors", McClelland and Stewart, Toronto: *The Canadian Publishers.*

Tuchman, Gaye (1978) "Making News: A Study in the Construction of Reality", Macmillan, New York: *The Free Press.*

Tversky, A. and Kahneman, D. (1974) "Judgment under Uncertainty: Heuristics and Biases", *Science* 185:1124-31 in Fischhoff, B., S. Read, and B. Combs (1978) "How Safe is Safe Enough?

U.S. News & World Report (1989) "Disturbing Numbers", 15 May, 106(19): 14(1).

Verhovek, Sam Howe (1999) "Across 10 Years, *Exxon Valdez* Casts a Shadow", *New York Times* (1999) 6 March, p. A1:A8.

Voke, Richard (1997) "SEVESO II, How will it affect Emergency Planning?", *From International Disaster and Emergency Response: IDER '97 Conference Proceedings.*

Webb, David A. (1994) "The Bathtub Effect: Why Safety Programs Fail", **Management Review**, February 83(2): 51-54.

Weick, K.E. (1990) "The Vulnerable System: An Analysis of the Tenerife Air Disaster", *Journal of Management*, in "From Bhopal to Banking: Organizational Design Can Mitigate Risk", pp. 571-593, Roberts and Libuser.

Weinberg, A. (1977) "Is Nuclear Energy Acceptable?", *Bulletin of the Atomic Scientists*, 33(4): 54-60.

Williams, T.M. and Davis, R.W. (1990) "Sea Otter Rehabilitation Program: 1989 *Exxon Valdez* Oil Spill", *International Wildlife Research*, in Estes, James A. (1991) "Catastrophes and Conservation: Lessons from Sea Otters and the *Exxon Valdez,*" *Science,* Vol. 254.

Wilkins, Lee and Patterson, Philip (1987) "Risk Analysis and the Construction of News", *Journal of Communication*, Summer.

Wills, Jonathan (1991) "Europe's answer to oil spills", *New Scientist* 18 May (p.36-38).

Wilson, Richard (1979) Analyzing the Daily Risks of Life, *Technology Review*, February.

Wilson, Richard and Crouch, E.A.C. (1987) "Risk Assessment and Comparisons: An Introduction" *Science*, April 17, Volume 236, pp. 267-270.

Wolfe, Douglas A., et. al. (1994) "The Fate of the Oil Spilled from the *Exxon Valdez*", *Environment, Science, Technology*, Vol. 28(13).

Wolfe, Morris (1985) "Jolts, The TV Wasteland and the Canadian Oasis", *James Lorimer & Company*, Toronto.

Yagoda, Ben (1990) "Cleaning up a dirty image", *Business Month*, April, pp. 48-51.

Yandle, Bruce (1992), "Environment and Efficiency Lovers", *Society*, 29(3): 23-32.

Zenker, Arnold (1983) "Mastering the Public Spotlight", *Dodd, Mead & Company*, New York.

ALLAN BONNER
BA, BEd, MA, MSc, Ph.D (Cand.)

Allan Bonner has coached approximately 15,000 senior executives to deal with some of the most controversial and public issues of our time. He has worked with heads of government, G7 and UN delegations, the WTO and NATO, as well as CEOs and diplomats around the world. He has recently worked in Hong Kong, Seoul, Tokyo, Bangkok, Beijing, Singapore, Canberra, Budapest, Geneva, most American states and all Canadian provinces.

In his 14-year career in journalism, he worked at the local and network levels in both Canada and the United States.

He holds university degrees in Political Science, Education, a Master's in Political Economy with a thesis on the media and an MSc in Risk, Crisis and Disaster Management. He taught journalism at the college level and has lectured on crisis management and media training by request at several universities and colleges, including the University of Toronto, York University and the Banff School of Advanced Management.
Mr. Bonner has been trained in Leadership Education and negotiation skills at Harvard University's John F. Kennedy School of Government. He is currently studying for a PhD in law.

Mr. Bonner has been a contributor to *Marketing Magazine, Law Times, Bout de Papier, Canadian Corporate Counsel,* and *Internal Communication Focus.*

Recent speaking engagements include The World Conference on Disaster Management, Canadian Public Relations Society, The Insight Conference on Crisis Communication and Risk Management, International Association of Business Communicators, the Tokyo and Princeton Chambers of Commerce, the Rhode Island Emergency Management Agency, The National Business Show, and the Emirates International Disaster and Environment Conference in Dubai.

Allan has been studying the martial arts and Eastern philosophy for eight years, and is making modest progress.

ALLAN BONNER COMMUNICATIONS MANAGEMENT INC.
The Centre For Training in Risk and Crisis Management
Phone 416-961-3620   Fax 416-961-4523   Toll Free 1-877-484-1667
e-mail: allan@allanbonner.com
web: www.allanbonner.com